Modernism and Hegemony

Theory and History of Literature
Edited by Wlad Godzich and Jochen Schulte-Sasse

For other books in the series, see p. 126.

Modernism and
Hegemony
A Materialist Critique of
Aesthetic Agencies

Neil Larsen
Foreword by Jaime Concha

Theory and History of Literature, Volume 71

University of Minnesota Press, Minneapolis

Published by the University of Minnesota Press
2037 University Avenue Southeast, Minneapolis, MN 55414.
Printed in the United States of America.

Library of Congress Cataloging-in-Publication Data

Larsen, Neil.
    Modernism and hegemony : a materialist critique of aesthetic
agencies / Neil Larsen.
        p.   cm. — (Theory and history of literature ; v. 71)
    Includes index.
    ISBN 0-8166-1784-8   ISBN 0-8166-1785-6 (pbk.)
    1. Modernism (Art) — Controversial literature. 2. Ideology.
3. Aesthetics, Modern — 20th century.   I. Title.   II. Series.
BH301.M54L37   1990
111'.85'0904 — dc20   89-30475
                                                             CIP

For Bea, Leonard, and Emma

"May this for which we dread to lose
Our privacy, need no excuse."

Contents

Acknowledgments

Wlad Godzich, Ron Sousa, Bob Krueger, Doris Sommer, Róger Zapata, and Román de la Campa all helped guide *Modernism and Hegemony* to completion, providing both inspiration and invaluable criticisms. My sincere thanks to them. I am also deeply and especially grateful to Holbrook Robinson of Northeastern University, whose support at a critical time assured completion of the present work.

Foreword
From the Modernism of Adorno to the Contemporaneity of Marx
Jaime Concha

Translated by Kitty Millet

Readers of the Theory and History of Literature series of the University of Minnesota Press are perhaps acquainted with Neil Larsen's foreword to Fredric Jameson's essays (vol. 48 of the series). There, in a lucid presentation, Larsen points out a central paradox about Jameson, author of *Marxism and Form* and *The Political Unconscious*: a Marxism without political practice and, as a consequence, a critical method that, because of its tendency to unify synthetically heterogeneous points of view, at times fails to criticize other methods that offer incompatible concepts of literature. Jamesonian metacommentary seems to situate itself far from real political life and beyond the polemical pugnaciousness one usually associates with Marxism. As early as his *Jena Dissertation* (1841), Marx writes,

> It's a psychological law that the theoretical mind, once liberated in itself, turns into a practical energy . . . but the practice of philosophy is itself theoretical. It's the critique that measures the individual existence by the essence.[1]

In Jameson's case, and in accordance with his procedure, structuralism and critical theory, for example, can conceive of themselves as moments of a micro-Hegelian process, which ends by subsuming them under a superior, interpretive code.[2] It is difficult to avoid verifying that, within this intellectual project, two of its complementary aspects are a purely theoretical Marxism and a somewhat omnivorous Hegelianism.

With a fairness and equanimity free from condemnation and the crude acceptance of facts, Larsen tries to determine the historical reasons and institutional circumstances that explain this situation, in which a vigorous and clearly renovative thinking gets trapped in an iron circle that robs its projection in the social sphere. At the root of everything, as Jameson himself notes in *Periodizing the 60s*,[3] lies a miniscule repression that took place soon after the middle of the century: the phenomenon of McCarthyism, the internal face of the country's international politics during the Cold War. This repression, which was televised as a case of individual pathology and collective hysteria, had enormous repercussions on the whole of North American society. Its engineering was perfect, to say the least. In the State's administrative sphere, it strikes first at the functionaries of the previous regime, who, thinking differently, had participated in a very different set of alliances during the war—something we are now pressured to erase from historical memory. The Hiss case is symptomatic in this respect. In the area of cultural activities and information, singularly aggressive attacks are leveled at filmmakers, playwrights, and progressive-thinking artists in general—not to mention the scientific establishment, especially the group of physicists tied to the development of atomic energy.[4] Among the many names one could mention, the Hollywood ten, Arthur Miller, and Oppenheimer become strongly illustrative. Finally, and ever more decisively, in the field of production and social struggle, the dismantling of the more class-conscious workers' organizations is achieved by means of blacklists, ideological persecution, and, not least, organized crime.[5] With a purged administration, an impoverished and domesticated cultural life,[6] and a seemingly pro-worker leadership controlled by employers, society was saved and could concentrate on the Korean war in order to enter some years later into the whirlwind of Vietnam. The fact that illustrious figures from the most recent decades, like Nixon and Reagan, launched their public careers at the height of McCarthyism, well illustrates the continuity and uniform character of North American political life in the second half of this century. In such a climate, the fact that Jameson, together with others (but Jameson above all in the humanities area), may have opened a space for Marxism and for authors like Sartre, Lukács, Bloch, Benjamin, Adorno, and Althusser, represents no small feat. One result of this opening: it is no longer considered "indecorous" to speak of ideology at the heart of the academy, and within the framework of literary studies, one can occasionally bring in "extra-literary" considerations.[7]

In applying a similar perspective to the author of the present book, I can fix his position, the material perspective from which he speaks, within three coordinates: teaching, the comparatist focus, and Larsen's interest in history and political events, in particular those of the United States and Latin America. A professor himself, he stipulates that the idea of confronting the texts of Adorno and Marx—a species of frictional reading constituting the base and nucleus of the first chapter—occurred first in the classroom. Comparatist by training, Larsen continues an orientation, untraditional in the discipline, of abandoning the persistent North-Occidental tropism that has characterized it (Western Europe, Anglo-Saxon countries, etc.). Finally, a marked valorization of political activism recurs in these pages, giving to some passages of his essay exceptional force (for example, when he writes of the television spectator confronting the violence in Central America). Of course, these determinations do not always operate positively. The comparatist gaze, to cite only a single case, is at times exacerbating, acquiring an uncontrollable movement, breaking what seems to me the dominant logic of the argument. In my opinion, the comparatist tic proves to be perceptibly inopportune at the end of Chapter 3, when the appeal to B. Traven emerges as a *deus ex machina* to contrast Traven's work, from a perspective that seems artificial, with the meaning and values of Rulfo's narrative. These variables, specifying an institutional locus, a methodological angle, and an ethical component, combine and weigh more or less heavily in various parts of the essay, resulting in a singularly complex contribution that inscribes itself in its own right in the contemporary debate on themes of ideological criticism.

Indeed, without a doubt, *Modernism and Hegemony* is a complex, even dense, book, not only because of the ambitiousness of its goals (the type of problems it addresses), not only because of the constant transgression of the established limits between disciplines, but above all because of the multiple analytic categories that Larsen's reflection sets in motion. With this in mind, I propose in this preface to offer a preliminary guide to the design of the book, to its logical structure, and to indicate some distinctive aspects of its theoretical contribution and its critical results. I will omit the introduction, which contains relatively independent developments suggestive enough that readers may have the pleasure of discovering them on their own.

I called the principal articulation of the first chapter a "frictional" reading. In effect, it has to do with the comparison between a section in *Minima Moralia* by Adorno and that exceptional text, fundamental to the thought of the nineteenth century, *The Eighteenth Brumaire of Louis Bonaparte*. A classic of revolutionary history (and of repressive tactics) at an early moment of the class struggle during the capitalist epoch, a cornerstone of political theory in general and of the State in particular, its pull has remained constant for almost a century and a half during which it has remained current.[8] Among other ways, its continuous impact is shown by its having elicited the commentary of a personality of world-historical significance (Lenin) and the assiduous meditations of men as diverse as Levi-Strauss and Kim Philby.[9] The choice of these texts could, then, seem disproportionate; and I confess my surprise when encountering it. How can Larsen justify integrating these two texts in the same "intertextual field?" Isn't that a relation between incommensurables, i.e., "irrational" in a mathematical sense? Nevertheless, as the principal line of argumentation became clear to me, the broad dialogical swatch that Larsen traces definitely began to make sense.

The reasoning proceeds more or less as follows: starting from the dichotomy between Realism and Modernism, a dichotomy that Jameson tends to historicize but whose aporetic character subsists *malgré-lui*, Larsen delimits a common ground in which such an antithesis is born and unfolds. This "ideological horizon" is none other than the sphere of representation or, rather, representability, since currently a crisis of representation exists, obliging one to ask oneself immediately: Is it possible to represent social truth? Can history be an object of representation?

One knows Adorno's answer, which Larsen recounts with detail and rigor, granting to the Frankfurt School philosopher the necessary benefit of the doubt: in the reign of total reification, in the world of the absolute without meaning (*pathos* belongs to an authentic jargon!), all realist art is condemned to fall repeatedly into general banality. Only a work of art that is pure negation can aspire to represent the ubiquitous and boundless abstraction of social substance — Adorno *dixit*.[10] Such is his Modernism: Beckett's farce or Kafka's universe. At the present time, the possibility of aesthetic representation grounds itself in the artwork's character of negation.

It is hard not to take into account here a biographical itinerary that could be summarized thus: Adorno lived under fascism, knew the consumer society of the Eastern and Western United States, and returned to live in post-Nazi and neo-Nazi Germany surrounded by an even worse consumerism.[11] This *Voyage au Bout . . . d'aujourd'hui* naturally gives rise to the verdict on social reality just noted. But what does it consist of, this representative negation that is the essential characteristic of the work of art? By formulating the question in this way, the reader can have the impression — as I did while reading Larsen's work — that there is a constant fluctuation of meaning in the key term of the exposition, that of representation. Although free of psychological connotations, the term "representation" has its philosophical center of gravity in its cognitive content. All the heritage — the weight and heaviness — of German idealism, which Adorno never overcame, is deposited in the notion of representation.[12] Later on, in the context created by the discussion of *The Eighteenth Brumaire*, the vocabulary will incidentally acquire a theatrical significance or, more notoriously, it will take on the value of a political representativeness. Although Larsen generally controls these fluctuations, they occasionally disturb the reader, creating a minor fringe of obscurities.

The retrospective bond with *The Eighteenth Brumaire* turns out to be advantageous, because it helps to illuminate the genesis and the context of the problems. The theatricality of history (tragedy/comedy) in no way prefigures the route into aesthetics, as one might imagine.[13] The version of *history as farce* pinpoints the problematic relationship (to say the least) of history with the present, whose explanation resides, according to the suggestive interpretation of the author, in Marx's recognition that a new principle has been established, emerging in

modern society for the first time. Certainly, Marx doesn't shy away from postu-
lating a historical subject: the proletariat that was routed in 1848 will time and
again undertake a "storming of the heavens," that is to say, of the fruits of the
earth. This is a heroic and collective subject that critical theory persists in ignor-
ing. In any case, the installation of Bonapartism implies something new, whose
distinctive character the Marxist analysis captures for the first time (in correla-
tion, that is, with passages of the *Grundrisse*.) In Bonaparte's usurpation of
power, which is the climax of the counterrevolutionary process, the State does
not represent the bourgeoisie directly: it represents it partially, but also sets itself
against the bourgeoisie, and does not cease combatting it. A principle of abstraction, the general and fetishized character of capital, acts and operates in this
asymmetry of representativeness (which I do not think should be exaggerated to
the point of questioning the classical theory of the relations between class and
State). In Larsen's literal formulation, one would have to do with "a superordinate social agency with no fixed political or cultural subjectivity." Adorno's view
of almost a century later, which will give nourishment to the unrestricted privilege of the Aesthetic, is here, in Marx's earlier text, proposed in its *political* basis, the proper and natural locus of the phenomenon and its problematic.
Adorno's version of Modernism is thus revealed to be incapable of transcending
reification; in fact, it participates in it and its ideological network. With that, two
important issues are introduced at the end of the chapter: the question of the
State, of power, arises, and quickly gives way in turn to the transpolitical dimension of hegemony; second, something already sketched in the introduction is
again taken up, a *leit-motif* in Larsen's point of view: the notion of inversion as
the primary and central factor in the Marxist conception of ideology.

I am not qualified, because I lack pictorial culture, to follow closely the contents of Chapter 2, which concentrates almost exclusively on certain works by
Manet. The facts are simple, in any case. On one side of the ocean, on Mexican
soil, the execution of Maximilian of Austria; on the other side of the Atlantic, in
France, Manet paints the event in a succession of "Modernist" paintings. What
is the meaning of this inter-continental correspondence?

In his commentary on *The Eighteenth Brumaire*, Larsen had already empha-
sized the exceptional form of Marx's journalism, where the facts, beyond their
anecdotal profile, were set out in an intelligible periodization to reveal their historical sense.[14] With respect to the paintings of Manet, the dilemma is a paradigm of the negation of history, according to the Modernist optic (Malraux,
Bataille, etc.), suggesting that *The Execution of Maximilian* is, as competent spe-
cialists have proved, also the serial product of news reports that were arriving in
Europe by wire some weeks after the event. Despite its dependence on the most
contingent actuality, the representation purportedly frees itself, to the point of
demonstrating a complete indifference before history, a liberation that would
make of it a truly modern and Modernist work of art: so says the legend that

Larsen then critiques. Such a close and decisive correspondence with the *fait divers* is, of course, conveniently ignored—disregarded, rather—in this Modernist reading of Manet's painting. Nonetheless:

> Sandblad's readings of the series of press reports show the existence of a rigid correspondence between the pictorial variations and the availability of additional information concerning the physical setting of the execution proper (35).

In this way, the constitutive seriality of the painting is shown not as an impossibility, or a disinterest in representing history, but rather as a continual search, "tantalizing" in the strongest sense of myth, after an understanding that is discovered to be necessarily incomplete in the face of the density of historical objectivity. This apparently "modernist" work conceals a deeply realist project, which will in the end be verified in the culminating work, *The Barricade*.

And even so, the dilemma does not reside uniquely in the genesis of the work and the artistic process as such: it is simultaneously transferred to the painting's destination, to its "reception" on the part of contemporary society and the State. To paint the death of Maximilian in the last days of the regime of Napoleon III, to whose collapse it greatly contributed, was not only a historical gesture but also a political act. Hence its exhibition is impeded, and, above all, its lithographic reproduction is prohibited; that is—as Larsen describes so well—the democratic diffusion of painting is especially restricted, a diffusion that threatens to remind the larger population of the sad and grotesque imperial adventure. The other version, the oil panting, can tranquilly remain in the museum. It is not dangerous, at least not directly or immediately.

The remaining essays transport us to Latin American regions, to Mexico and Brazil to be precise. Continuing his procedure of conceptualizing the miniscule, Larsen now reflects on a story of Juan Rulfo, "La cuesta de las comadres," from *El Llano en Llamas*. In a critical dialogue with the previous valorizations and explications of Rulfo's work (those that Larsen designates as "left-oriented" as well as the transcultural criticism of Angel Rama), the author proposes his own analysis, which aspires to account for the flagrant absence of the determinations of the State in the Rulfian scenario and narrative. It is this vacuum of hegemony, this evacuation of its problematic determinations, that gives the narrative strategy of Rulfo an affinity and bond with Modernist aesthetics.

Now, although it may be possible to agree in principle with the circles drawn to facilitate an understanding of the Mexican author (the post-revolutionary epoch, the politics of *alemanismo*, demobilization of intellectuals, etc.), it is rather difficult to accept the following:

> This much, we think, can be stated without equivocation: Rulfo's transcultural modernization of Mexican and Latin American traditions of

narrative is progressive in the precise degree that the broader hegemonic
transformation which endows Rulfian narrative with its particular
'subject effect' can be similarly characterized (68).

Permit me to disagree: the parallelism is not convincing, nor would such a
proposition resolve the problem if it were, since this "precise degree" to which
Larsen refers is the great enigma of Latin American development. It is not the
best tactic to respond to a problem with an even greater one.

Finally, Brazil—the classic site of South American exoticism. Here, the author analyzes cultural creations that include the literary avant-garde of the
twenties—the so-called Brazilian Modernism—and some of the more recent ex-
pressions of *Cinema Novo*, which, after the impact-producing films in its first
epoch, undergo commercialization and co-optation by ideological mechanisms of
the State (the cinematic versions of Amado's novels represent this phase well). In
a particularly ingenious manner, Larsen opposes the aesthetics of "expropriation" and of "consumptive production" elaborated by Oswaldo de Andrade in
his manifestos *Pau Brasil* (1924) and *Antropofagia* (1928), with the emblem of
"hunger," promoted years later by the cineaste Glauber Rocha, establishing a
continuity in the underlying ideological process and, at the same time, the frac-
ture caused by the Brazilian crisis. Clearly, the optimistic resolution of the indig-
enous/foreign antithesis, such as it was proposed in the effervescent atmosphere
of the avant-garde, gives way afterward to the brutal irruption of negativity—the
dry, harsh edge of want that the cinema tries to project as its artistic-social effect.
The factors at play are multiplied here almost beyond measure, including a partial refutation of (Adornian disciple) Roberto Schwarz's standpoint, focusing on
the "mass snobbism" fomented by the populist State. Although the cohesion of
the reasoning sometimes escapes me, one does find the book returning to its fundamental critical theme: Adorno's inability (or that of his disciples) to account
objectively for the Modernist phenomenon. What in Adorno's theorizing took the
form of an antithesis between a pure and disinterested work of art, on the one
hand, and, on the other, a "culture industry" administered by the State, is shown
to be—now, in the Brazilian cultural process—two branches of the same development. Artistic autonomy and mass manipulation are no longer opposing poles,
but, rather, the avatars of something that was believed and judged to be free at
first but that ends up completely dependent on state control. In this way, the intimate nature of Modernism, which escapes Adorno in the domains of the metropolis, reveals its shameful truth at the periphery, on the margins where the
mechanisms and the power of big capital are drawn out.

If we now stand back to consider my schematic and oversimplified commentary, some points call attention to themselves. These points are not reservations,
much less objections; they are only aspects that seem to me worth noting and that
might provide material for subsequent reflection. Needless to say, I apologize to

the author and to his readers in the not improbable event that I have misunderstood some of the ideas on which I have commented. I will proceed from the minor to the major points.

(1) *The modernist canon.* The author works with a very broad concept of modernism that tends to weaken its operative validity. After more than a century and a wide variety of aesthetic developments, can there be one valid term for this huge domain of time and space? There is something futile about reducing such disparate manifestations to a single category. Certainly, the minimum corpus, the rather amorphous canon, with which Larsen works finds its justification in the fact that what interests him is its philosophical version, the conceptualization of modernism in Adorno's theory. However, in this connection, the Latin American exhibits are crucial to an evaluation of *Modernism and Hegemony*. If his concept of Modernism as applied to Brazilian art forms turns out to be sensible and functional, I do not believe the same is true for Rulfo. Rulfo, a modernist? I believe that Rulfo would have been the first to be surprised by this label. ''This was in old times,'' begins the analyzed story, at the end of the first paragraph of ''La cuesta de las comadres''. And, as in all of Rulfo's densely concentrated narrative, the entire story is traversed by the ubiquitous and omnipresent problem of the land. Land is an archaism: everything conspires to make one doubt any understanding of Rulfo as a modernist. Neither the historical context, Rulfo's peculiar regionalism, nor even the spirit of the narrative techniques put into practice seems to support Larsen's conceptualization, which I consider somewhat forced.

(2) *The element of the aesthetic.* A component central to Larsen's discourse is the critique of the privilege attributed by Adorno to the aesthetic. In critical theory, the aesthetic hypertrophies, acquiring a status of political *Ersatz* in relation to contemporary society. Nevertheless, although this is undoubtedly the case, the notion of the aesthetic does not seem to me worked out from within, following the rigorous and complex steps that have been elaborated in Adorno's philosophy. Not to belabor the obvious, it is still worth remembering that the aesthetic has an older dynamism in Adorno's thought, a dynamism that dates back more or less to his book on Kierkegaard, curiously never mentioned by Larsen.[15] And this is not *Vorgeschichte*. On the contrary: from this early coexistence of the aesthetic with ethical and religious stages of existence, which Adorno explored and criticized in the Danish thinker, there derives a conceptual coefficient which makes it impossible for it to be reduced to the apolitical, to that which is antipolitical, or to the simple dissimulation of the political (these being degrees and nuances with which the author presents the aesthetic). Precisely because Adorno opposes the inferior status that Kierkegaard assigns to the aesthetic, it takes on a density and values that allow it to represent social negation, to become the possible correlate of the negated and negative totality; in this way, it acquires a supra-political projection, to the extent that it puts into relief the limitations of the political as such, and of empirical politics in the narrow sense. The backdrop, of course, is nothing other

than that of totalitarian capitalism (= fascism) or of society where the domination of the principle of exchange value has arrived as its extreme limits (= X?).

(3) *Latin American violence*. In his observations concerning Rulfo's short story, Larsen seems to suggest that the actions narrated there could be read under the aegis of Latin American violence, where it is seen as a sign and expression of a barbaric subcontinent. I think he fails to perceive the essential: a phenomenon—whose character is not regional but world-historical—and that moreover traverses the entire map and every plane of our cultural experience. Consider only what pertains to the domains of literature: would the violence of Latin American literature have here a differential index of barbarism, and why should this violence be seen as distinct from the succulent massacres of Homer or Shakespeare, or the bloody excesses of Aeschylus or Dante? In one not negligible sense, all Western literature is nothing but a grand thematization of violence— whatever attitude might be taken with respect to it or derived from it. On these matters, as in others, everything seems to have started with the intrigues outside Troy. Perhaps it is this, and not a theological disgust, which awakened the holy irritation of Heraclitus, when, in one of the fragments that has been little clarified, it is attributed to him that "he declared Homer worthy of being ejected from the debates and thrashed."[16] Therefore, it is better to end this line of discussion and dispense once and for all with the commonplace of Latin American violence. (Of course, Larsen's ideas are subtle: what he is, indeed, criticizing is an aesthetization of violence that he perceives in Rulfo's narrative.)

(4) *Ideological inversion*. In a sustained and very conscious exposition, from the introduction to the final pages, the relation of inversion is considered to be the definitive trait of ideology in the Marxist perspective. It is curious to observe that the foreword to Jameson's volume, already mentioned, also closes with a reference to the *camera obscura*—the pregnant and resonating image with which Marx crystallizes his analysis in *The German Ideology*. Nevertheless, despite the power and validity of the image, it is convenient to take into account the place of the notion in Marx's evolution and not to forget that there are other aspects which interact significantly in this important and controversial formulation.

It is evident that the relation of inversion (*Umkehrung*) is the philosophical result of a first step in Marx's thought, which runs from 1841 to 1845, and that it is tied to other conceptual components which became quickly submerged in his foregoing evolution. First source: theological alienation in Feuerbach's sense, a true embryo of inversion; second step: critical displacement against neo-Hegelian speculation, in the particular conditions of Germany; third moment: abstraction and generalization, which permits Marx to determine the relation between the juridico-political and cultural spheres and the material base as represented inversely in consciousness, etc. In a sort of *raccourci*, these poles appear condensed in the first section of *The German Ideology* (which not by chance figures in the manuscript under the name of Feuerbach!), but they had already been anticipated, in a wavering and fascinating way, in that notable early text, the "Introduction to the Critique of Hegel's *Philosophy of Right*."[17] Along a broken and complex path, always opposing the political situation of France to Germany's historical underdevelopment, Marx here definitively breaks the Hegelian homogeneity between the particular and the universal, to show, through these determinations of the concept, the social contradictions (of the family and civil society with the State, of the particular classes with society in its entirety, etc.). This dialectic between the partial (*partiel, besondres*) and the universal (*universelles, allgemeines*) will be historicized succinctly in *The German Ideology* (separation of the manual and intellectual forms of labor, opposition of country versus city, etc.), to prepare for the profound study — which today we consider simple because we have so fundamentally internalized it — of the relation between the ideas of the dominant class and the whole of society. Here before us is the fundamental ideological operation: the fictitious universalization of particular interests. Thus, the private property of a few is proposed as also sacred to the dispossessed majority; the *American way of life* becomes established as the ideal life for all the inhabitants of the metagalaxy, etc. This conception of ideology based on the Hegelian triad is not incompatible with the other one, the one governed by the inversion on which Larsen puts greater emphasis, but it doesn't always coincide with it and seems to me endowed by a richer potentiality in the subsequent thought of Marx.

****

At a conference on the principles of 68, held under the auspices of a Hegelian Seminar directed by Jean Hyppolite in the College of France, Althusser sustained the following:

> The union, or fusion of the workers' movement and Marxist theory is the greatest event of the history of class societies, that is to say practically of all human history.[18]

In the contemporary philosophical climate, in the midst of the panorama of the last few years, those accents sound strange, endowed as they are with a faith and a rotundity that today are unacceptable to many. A generalized "anti-Hegelianism" currently dominates many areas of knowledge, in many university circles.[19] Now, as on other occasions, the struggle against Hegel is the oblique disqualification of Marx and of the historico-practical fruits of Marx's influence on the planet; on other occasions, as also now, the intent of going further than Hegel is really an attempt to return to pre-Hegelian philosophy:[20] a return to Kant (J.-L. Nancy) or to Fichte (A. Philonenko). In the better known case of Deleuze, the attack is directed against the thought of identity and contradiction, his *bête noire* being none other than the negation of the negation, in opposition to which arises the apparent radicalism of difference, repetition, simulacra, etc. Uncritical thought, yet "diacritical" in a strict sense, in spite of its incidental recourse to sophisticated mathematical entities ("differential" from calculus, topological variations, etc.), it relapses into the banal equation of variety and of pluralism, this latter brandishing itself—ideologically—as an antidote against the perversions of the system, of totality and whatever type of holism. Against this intellectual background, Larsen's contribution acquires a singular interest and significance.

In various of its facets, *Modernism and Hegemony* is a typical and representative book of the current decade, of the mid to late eighties. Only one characteristic: the abundance, almost proliferation, of theory. This aspect brings to mind the curious associations with which Jean Wahl defines the term in his original philosophical dictionary:

> Abundance. . . . I never liked abundance very much. There is in the idea of abundance, an idea of an absence of obstacles, of difficulties.[21]

There is some truth in this statement. With respect to the field of literary studies, the presumed "literary theories" have little that is theoretical and, often, nothing to do with literature. Larsen's work shares this interest in theory, yet it never makes his ideas vacuous, scholastic. Rather than vaporous speculations amounting to little "machines that function in a vacuum" (Dilthey's phrase, which he was applying to grand metaphysical systems), there is in the present analysis a search for solidity, to the extent that Larsen aspires to reactivate the roots of the Marxist inheritance. And that desired reactivation confers on his contribution an exceptional value.

For very comprehensible reasons, academic Marxism has had to define itself in the United States through opposition to "vulgar" Marxism, in order that it not be confused with positions that obviously do not enjoy official sympathy or, much less, state protection. In this there is a self-defensive reflex that is easy to understand. A label like that of "neo-Marxism," with which the historical-materialist method found entry and early legitimation in the academy, is in itself revelatory. The other Marxism, the bad Marxism, besides being "vulgar," stands condemned as a "paleo-Marxism," an ancient form of conceiving social and cultural analysis. Nevertheless, to escape from one vice frequently means adopting an opposite one: in this case, the elitist deformation of Marxism. Vulgar Marxism, elitist Marxism: two faces, if you will, of the same defect of unilaterality. Unilateral emphasis on the economic, unilateral emphasis on the cultural. Or, to use a political vocabulary: an overestimation of the economic struggle in one case and an overestimation of the ideological struggle (methodologies, etc.) on the other. Thus one of the principal merits of Larsen's essay is to be conscious of the dilemma and to seek the sources, that is, the very texts of Marx, for the integrated and dialectical vision of social phenomena. In the antipodes of the reigning anti-Hegelianism, rather than a return to a pre-Hegelian epoch, this book proposes—simply but decisively—a return to Marx, to the validity of his texts and to the fully contemporaneous spirit of his method of cultural analysis.

San Diego, 1989

Notes

1. "The Difference between the Democritean and Epicurean Philosophies of Nature," in *Collected Works of Karl Marx and Frederick Engels*, vol. 1 (New York: International Publishers, 1975), p. 85.

2. In the present book, the author comments on another example, that of the triad constituted by Lukácsian realism, Brecht's Modernism, and Modernism according to Adorno. (See this same prologue, *infra*.)

3. F. Jameson, *The Ideologies of Theory: Essays 1971–1986*, vol. 2 (Minneapolis: University of Minnesota Press, 1988), pp. 178–208.

4. For a recent treatment of the Oppenheimer and other cases, see Daniel J. Kevles, *The Physicists: The History of a Scientific Community in Modern America* (Cambridge: Harvard University Press, 1987).

5. Cf. Herbert Morais and Richard O. Boyer: *La Historia Desconocida del Movimiento Obrero de los Estados Unidos* (Mexico: Editorial Solidaridad, 1984), pp. 459ff. (The original edition in English is from 1955.)

6. To the foreign observer, the culture and intellectual life of the first half of the century appear to possess greater density and solidity. Such figures as Edmund Wilson, Lewis Mumford, and Kenneth Burke prove, in spite of all their differences, to be equally rooted in and in contact with the problems of their country.

7. See Don Wayne, "Power, Politics, and the Shakespearean Text: Recent Criticism in England and the United States," in *Shakespeare Reproduced*, ed. by Jean E. Howard and Marion F. O'Connor (New York/London: Methuen, 1987), pp. 47–67. Wayne evaluates the change that has occurred in a particularly conservative sector of the academic establishment.

8. In her celebrated speech before the London Congress of Russian Social Democrats (1907), Rosa Luxemburg summarized in an impeccable manner the contents of *The Eighteenth Brumaire* and, in general, of the extracted teachings of Marx from 1848 and its results. (Cf. Raya Dunayevskaya, *Rosa Luxemburg, the Feminine Liberation and Marxist Philosophy from the Revolution*, (Mexico: FCE, 1985), pp. 37–38 and "Appendix," p. 394. (In English, 1981.)

9. Cf. C. Levi-Strauss, *Tristes Tropiques* (Paris: Plon, 1955), p. 62; and Kim Philby, *My Silent War* (Granada: Pantheon Books, 1969).

10. The formulas that Adorno coins are very expressive of his philosophical style: *Unmenschlichkeit der Geschichte, Unwesen* (non-essence, lack of essence), *Abstraktheit*, which implies, in fact, a double abstraction, a potentiality of the Abstract (*Gesammelte Schriften*, vol. 4, [Frankfurt: Suhrkamp, 1980], pp. 161–62.)

11. A concise and synthetic exposition of his life and work can be found in Martin Jay, *Adorno* (Cambridge: Harvard University Press, 1984).

12. For some observations concerning the protean aspect of notion in German Idealism, and, above all, in Hegel, cf. J. Derrida, "Le Puits et la Pyramide. Introduction a la Semiologie de Hegel," in *Hegel et la pensee moderne*, J. D'Hondt ed. (Paris: PUF, 1970), especially pp. 36 and 45ff.

13. The last statement is obviously out of focus. As far as I know, there does not seem to be sufficient clarity concerning the *status* of Marx's historical comparisons between tragedy and comedy. Sociologists discard them as mere rhetoric; Larsen assigns them an allegorical role, debatable, to

say the least. Whatever might be the status and real significance of these similes, it is good to remember that they appear already in the *Einleitung* (see further, note 17), tied to the anachronism of German history. One could thus think that comedy is symbolic of anachronism. But, from his Greek studies, comedy also represents for Marx (via Hegel) the moment of dissolution of historical forms. Summing up both connections, it is possible to infer that the analogy with comedy permits Marx to characterize a history that is falsified, whether because it is anachronistic or decadent—or as being both things at the same time. In fact, in *The Eighteenth Brumaire*, anachronism and decadence intermingle at the debut of a history that has already slipped out of the hands of the bourgeoisie: fleeing toward the proletariat and toward Bonapartism.

14. In *History of Economic Analysis* (New York: Oxford University Press, 1954), the economist Joseph Schumpeter, incisive critic of Marx, although capable of valorizing the profound merits of his social analysis, denotes this as the "transformation of historical narrative into historical reason."

15. Theodor Wiesengrund Adorno, *Kierkegaard. Konstruktion des Aesthetischen* (Tübingen: Mohr Verlag, 1933). See especially his specifications on the significations of the aesthetic (pp. 13ff. passim).

16. The fragment, number 42, is taken from Diogenes Laercio. (Cf. Rodolfo Mondolfo, *Heraclitos. Textos y problemas de su interpretacion*. [Mexico: Siglo XXI Editores, 8th ed., 1986], p. 36.)

17. There are more things in the *Einleitung* friend Marxist than the Marxologues have wanted to recognize, obsessed as they are by the desire to conceive of Marx's development as a rigid journey through previously determined spheres: the philosophical, the judicial, the political, the economical, etc. (I myself have just finished committing this sin, but consciously and because of constrictions of time and space.) This attitude is shared by a Marxist-Leninist like A. Cornu, in his decisive contributions concerning Marx and Engels, and by a Jesuit, like Jean Calvez, whose important monograph *La Pensée de Karl Marx* (Seuil, 1956) has been the basis for a Christian-Democratic reading of Marx. But if one attends to the images and expressive style, one will note in the *Einleitung* a conceptual dynamism in which is already anticipated the presence of a specter that opens *The Communist Manifesto* and the analogy between pseudo-history and comedy which begins *The Eighteenth Brumaire*. In the introduction, *Revenant y Komodie* are still figures of German anachronism.

18. L. Althusser: "Sur le rapport de Marx a Hegel," in *Hegel et la pensée moderne*, p. 87.

19. The formula is from G. Deleuze in *Différence et Répétition* (Paris: PUF, 1968) ab initio; but before that, in *Nietzsche and Philosophy* (1962), he was developing the same motif. (See J. Wahl's criticism of this last book, where he notes "a certain ill humor . . . against Hegelianism," *Revue de Metaphysique et de Morale*, June-Sept. 1963, p. 370.) It would be a question, then, in the case of Deleuze, of an ill-humored anti-Hegelianism!

20. This is one of the principal theses of the great work of G. Lukás, *The Destruction of Reason* (1952). For a reevaluation of this "bad" book in the Lukácsian bibliography, cf. Nicolas Tertulian, "La Destruction de la Raison—trente ans apres," in *Reification et Utopie: Ernst Bloch et Gyorgy Lukács un Siécle Apres*, (Editions Actes Sud, 1986), pp. 162–81.

21. J. Wahl, *Poesie, Pensée, Perception* (Calmann-Levy, 1948), p. 252.

Introduction

The four essays that comprise *Modernism and Hegemony* were either written or conceived during a period (the early 1980s) in which what some might now describe as the dissolution of high modernism was undergoing a "trickle down" into the provincial and proletarian strata of the humanities. *Modernism and Hegemony* can perhaps be read symptomatically as reflecting this moment, to the degree that it posits modernism itself, at least implicitly, as a broadly ideological signifier indicating not only the literary-artistic canon but a whole array of theoretical discourses from aesthetics to philosophy, culture, and politics. Modernism's breakup is now openly declared under the sign of the postmodern—a still volatile, contested, and uncertain epochal marker but one that nevertheless has the advantage of making it more difficult for modernism to avoid ideological detection by means of certain purely descriptive alibis. Postmodernism has, perhaps fortuitously, enabled us to perceive the central and apparently limiting modernist concern for aesthetics as itself a philosophical and political stance.

Modernism and Hegemony, then, might be said to stem from a postmodern conjuncture. But postmodernism describes not just this conjuncture and not even simply the theory that what emerges from the breakup of modernism may be a new (postmodern) cultural logic—it also has come to denote a particular ideological inflection within critical theory as a whole. Encompassing much of poststructuralism and including recent works by Lyotard, Baudrillard, Rorty, Laclau, and Mouffe, among others, this inflection has traced in the cultural shifts of the postmodern the corroborating signs of a deeper epistemological change. For Lyotard this entails the end of the tradition of legitimating knowledge in terms of "metanarratives"; for Laclau and Mouffe, the final break with the "essentialism" and "foundationalism" of the Enlightenment.

Modernism and Hegemony betrays little, if any, declared affinity for this direction in critical theory, in part at least because it hesitates before the premise that modernism has fully relinquished its intellectual and cultural hegemony. Moreover, *Modernism and Hegemony*—although sharing the postmodern perception of modernism as a discourse that has for too long been granted the privilege of "criticizing" itself from within the boundaries of its own ideological premises—proposes a number of theoretical conclusions that diverge significantly from the current thinking of postmodernist theory. It seems a matter of some importance, then, given the presently high level of interest evoked both by theories of the postmodern and by the postmodernization of theory, to sketch, in light of postmodern developments, the critique of modernism proposed here.

I

Modernism and Hegemony propounds, in the broadest and most schematic sense, a critical reading of high modernism as ideology according to the classically Marxist concept of inversion. As articulated most memorably in *The German Ideology* (and retained, with increasingly precise reformulations, throughout the writings of Marx and Engels), this figure entails the conception of ideology as the "inverted" consciousness determined by what is itself an inverted social and historical reality. Thus the capitalist market, a real set of relations, inverts the underlying reality of production relations by giving the appearance of a free and equal interaction to what is at base an unequal, coerced process of exploitation. The thinking of this reality that fails to reflect the specifically inverse connection between appearance and essence—as in utilitarianism and classical liberalism—counts as ideological.

What then is the inverted reality upon which is built the purportedly inverted thinking of modernism? To proceed at all along these lines, we must first grant to modernism itself the status of a *thinking* with some basis in objective social appearance. As I have already observed, postmodernism has produced the useful side-effect of framing modernism in this way—of refusing to be limited at the outset by modernism's own seemingly objective appearance as a set of sheerly literary and artistic methods. Here we may note as well that the Lukácsian critique of modernism, although successful in extrapolating from modernist artistic method certain political and generally ideological "equivalents" (as, for example, in the equation of the aesthetics of German expressionism with the ideology of petit-bourgeois pacifism and reformism in the World War I period),[1] ultimately regards these artistic features as the symptoms of a "decadence," that is, of an increasingly subjectivized, cognitively null form of consciousness. While I by no means dispute the conclusions drawn by Lukács vis-à-vis aesthetics in such writings as "The Ideology of Modernism"—a point on which I undoubtedly part company with both modernist and postmodernist theory alike—it is nevertheless true that this particular meaning of "ideology" leaves out of account precisely that extra-aesthetic content of modernism that the perspective of our present cultural and political scene brings into view.[2]

My thesis in *Modernism and Hegemony* is that modernism, as an ideology dominated by but not specific to the realm of aesthetics, is the inversion (the "inverted consciousness") of a historically objective "crisis in representation" affecting the construction of what are initially social and political identities. This crisis, I further speculate, is the result of the modernization of capital itself during the nineteenth century, especially in the period leading up to the transformation of "classical" free market capitalism into monopoly/state capitalism and imperialism. Marx grasped the essence of this development, I believe, in the tendency for capital in its real abstraction to break free from certain specific political—and in this sense, representational—relations and structures that were the condition of its initial autonomy and, thereby, to take on the attributes of a superordinate social agency with no fixed political or cultural subjectivity.[3] Thus the "crisis in representation" also entails a "crisis in agency": the sense that social and historical agency is exercised by subjects linked to society as a whole by representational bonds of identity—what we might characterize, using the contemporary jargon, as an epical "master narrative" or "grand narrative" of History—falters in the face of events that indicate that the traditional "heroes" have been usurped by anonymous forces. Modernism stems from this crisis— which it in turn grasps as stemming from an intrinsic falsity residing in a purely conceptual operation, representation—and inverts it. The crisis *in* representation becomes a crisis *of* representation: representation no longer "works," no longer appears to offer the subject any cognitive access to the object.

But modernism is not ready to relinquish the epical master narrative that is now threatened with dissolution. Agency must be retained, despite its apparent evacuation of the political. It is at this point, then, that modernism lays hand to the *aesthetic* and specifically to the (modern) 'work of art,' which alone among the postpolitical or subpolitical practices appears to hold out the promise of an oppositional synthesis. The very fact of its prior grounding in a "pure" practice of representation, a representation that enjoys a grant of autonomy from the object, is what appears to enable the aesthetic to transcend the fall of representation as the basis for the formation of subjects/agents. "Works of art" do not suddenly acquire autonomy in 'modern' times. This they have enjoyed in all traditional aesthetic philosophies at least since Kant. What they acquire—partly as a result of this autonomy, this initial separation from the fallen world of objects and practices—is the opportunity for "standing in," for occupying the lost terrain of social representation without falling to either side. Why, then, should they not stand in as well for the "lost" historical agency?

It is this peculiar logic of ascribing historical agency to aesthetic works and practices that, in my view, becomes the common thread of modernist ideology, including the avant-garde.[4] "Works of art" become the conceptual inversions of historical aporias, conceptual forms of anticapital. The crucial point here is that modernism is misapprehended as a strictly aesthetic "revolution," as a "challenge" to traditional aesthetics. The "aesthetic" operates as the signified of modernism, not as its signifier. Paraphrasing Walter Benjamin, we might term modernism an "aestheticization of the historical," a postpolitical reepicalization of historical metanarratives. On this point, at least, we can agree with Lyotard.

Here I must caution the reader that the ideology critique of modernism summarized above is the result neither of some comprehensive empirical sifting of documents nor of a rigorously scientific critique in the manner of *Capital*; rather, it is the speculative outcome of an experimental cross-reading of two theoretical discourses—Marxism and modernism—as they are embodied in two texts: Marx's *The Eighteenth Brumaire of Louis Bonaparte* and a selection from T. W. Adorno's *Minima Moralia* (fragment 94, "All the World's Not a Stage"). My initial decision to juxtapose these two texts (circumstantially the outcome of a comparative literature seminar that I attended as a graduate student) did not stem from any preconceived objective of proving or demonstrating a theory so much as from a suspicion that the concern of both Marx and Adorno to map the flight of the historical object—from the standpoint of revolutionary politics, for Marx; from that of aesthetics, for Adorno—would reveal a deeper, nonfortuitous connection.

My reading of Adorno in the course of carrying out this intertextual approach to modernism and the "crisis in representation" only served to confirm an initial conviction that in Adornian Critical Theory—as, to a somewhat less systematic degree, in the parallel and collaborative writings of Horkheimer and Marcuse— essentially what we have is modernism articulated in its purest, most fully theoretical, and at the same time most radical form. Adornian aesthetic theory is, if one likes, modernism in full conceptual regalia. Here, I think, the "aesthetization of the historical" continues to operate as the ideological horizon of theory, including social theory; nevertheless, the virtue of Adornian aesthetics is that, despite this inversion, the *objectivity* of the crisis in representation—the fact that it springs, even if inexplicably, from the historical object—is never relinquished. Ultimately, as I shall argue in the concluding section of Chapter 1, Adorno succumbs to a position of idealism. But Adorno's is—to use a conventional philosophical term—an objective idealism. The logic of Adornian critique is finally to invert, rather than collapse, being and consciousness in the manner of the classically idealist systems: a melancholized Hegelianism.

2

Thinking of Adorno in this way, it is then possible to observe how certain prominent developments in postmodern theory give the appearance of overcoming the Adornian/modernist inversion. I will limit myself here to the discussion of two such developments, which seem to bear close affinity: Lyotard's notion of "paralogy" in *The Postmodern Condition* and Ernesto Laclau and Chantal Mouffe's theory of "hegemony" developed in their *Hegemony and Socialist Strategy*.

Lyotard's arguments in *The Postmodern Condition* have become a well-known landmark in contemporary debates over the postmodern, particularly in the context of his polemic against the promodernist stance of Habermas. Here the crisis in representation/agency is formulated in terms of narrative—"grand" and "small"—and the problem of legitimation: the fall of representation is presented as the collapse of directly narrative knowledge. Modernism, understood here in an almost exclusively scientific-epistemological sense, defines a type of knowledge that has pushed the "grand narratives" to the margins, where, as "metanarratives," they nevertheless continue to function as an ultimate court of appeals, legitimating the various modernist practices when their *ends* as such are questioned. Thus the category of "historical agency"—the effect of a grand narrative of History—can no longer be thought as embodying itself directly in events. Modernist knowledge, even if it must finally sanction itself in the same grand narrative as something "meta," can think the category itself only as fictional. A spontaneous identity of agency and History presupposes the prelapsarian unity of narrative knowledge with its object—that is, presupposes representation.

Lyotard then poses the postmodern as a complex transformation comprising a generalized "incredulity towards metanarratives" along with a return to directly narrative knowledge on a strictly "heteromorphous" level. Like the traditional knowledge carried by grand narratives, the knowledge that "small narratives" bear "does not give priority to the question of its own legitimation and . . . certifies itself in the pragmatics of its own transmission."[5] But the practice of small narratives, unlike that of the traditional form, does not posit its own end as residing in the object of narrative cognition, with which it is thought to be finally identical or transparent. Small narrative retains the "unity of tradition" but aims only to perpetuate itself, or—in the manner of Richard Rorty, a kindred thinker—to "keep the conversation going."[6] The Habermasian telos of consensus implies a relapse into fixity—representation—that could only once again seek its legitimacy outside itself. "Pragmatic certification" requires, against this, a movement toward *dissension*, the negative impulse that enables the production of "new statements," the changing of the rules of the (language) game. This ceaselessly self-generative and self-displacing locally dispersed form of small narrative knowledge is the practice that Lyotard calls *"paralogy."*

In a foreword to the English translation of Lyotard's work, Fredric Jameson observes that in this final valorization of the innovative there is enacted a return to a classically modernist fixation.[7] Be this as it may, however, we must take note of a crucial difference here: the negative, transformative, or simply critical impulse no longer, as for modernism, pertains to the transsubjective abstraction of the "work" but, rather, to the seemingly concrete, historically situated, and practical subject of paralogy. Of course, this subject preserves a similarly formal abstractness, in line with Lyotard's poststructuralist adherences. But unlike its aestheticized modernist ancestor, it appears to have regained the terrain of the practical and contingent—the postmodernist "everyday"—without falling back into a representational fixation. Whereas the modernist agency is remote and esoteric, paralogy seems rooted in experience; whereas the "work of art" can exercise its critical faculty only against the bad society as a whole, at its uppermost limits of total reification, the subverting activity of paralogy can direct itself at virtually any local "discursive practice." The slogan of "local determinism," then, should be taken here not only as an anti-"totalitarian" measure but as part of a conceptual drive to construct a new locus of postmodern agency.

This migration toward the contingent and quotidian may be thought of as reflected in a movement from aesthetics per se—the privileged philosophical discourse of modernism—to the central postmodernist philosopheme of *ethics*. Lyotard thus retains from the Habermasian project the idea of justice, albeit one "not linked to [the idea and practice] of consensus."[8] Even if paralogy aims to change the rules of the game in the midst of play, these rules *"must* be local, . . . agreed on by . . . present players and subject to eventual cancellation."[9]

But what, we may ask, of the "language game" that is power itself? On this question Lyotard's theoretical efforts seem to collide rather clumsily with a conventional liberalism that is just barely avoided in the course of the principal argument. If agency is to be brought back to earth from its aesthetic heaven, should not the object of this grounding be a reencounter with the *political* rather than simply some abstract notion of fair play?

This brings us to *Hegemony and Socialist Strategy*, which may be read as roughly the effort to extend the concept of paralogy, or a semiotic agency grounded in actual discursive practice, beyond the confines of the "game" in Lyotard's ethical sense and into the "discursive field" of power relations. *Hegemony and Socialist Strategy* is a work of occasionally forbidding complexity that I cannot pretend to recapitulate fully or assess in the present space. Its general ideological and intellectual import, however, cannot seriously be doubted and it may well be considered a culmination not only of the postmodernist road to "politics" via Lyotard but of a self-referential series of poststructuralist attempts to trace the route from deconstruction and the critique of the sign into some new Marxian/post-Marxian vision of revolutionary strategy.[10]

Laclau and Mouffe begin by tracing the genealogy of the concept of hegemony as it emerges from what they term the "crisis of Marxism" instigated by the capitalist crisis of 1873–96 and the emergence of monopoly capitalism and imperialism. The effect of the crisis is, in the authors' view, to undermine the base/superstructure theory and the belief in the necessity of proletarian revolution that stems from it. Confronted with an "autonomization of spheres" and an overall "opacity of the social," the orthodox Marxism of the Second International is forced to search for ways to assimilate theoretically the new realities (Laclau and Mouffe are never overly precise as to what these are) without abandoning the 'essentialist' and teleological standpoint of orthodoxy itself.[11] Thus, for example, the concept of hegemony is developed by Russian social democracy to account for the evident strategic necessity for the proletariat to carry out the "bourgeois-democratic" tasks that the Russian bourgeoisie itself, because of its uneven development, is unable to perform. Hegemony is logically conceived as "supplemental."

It is this "supplemental," strictly temporary, and contingent hegemony that, when joined to the Sorelian theory of the "revolutionary bloc," results in the more familiar Gramscian use of the concept. Gramscian hegemony in fact denotes what Laclau and Mouffe pronounce to be a new "political logic," in which revolution itself ceases to be warranted by the "laws of history" and must be the outcome of actively constructing hegemonic unity among and across class subjects.

But even the Gramscian theory suffers from a residual "essentialism," for it still asserts that it is the "ontologically privileged" class—whether bourgeoisie or proletariat—that acts as the agent/beneficiary of hegemony. In reality, argue Laclau and Mouffe, "the identity of classes is transformed by the hegemonic tasks" (*HSS*, p. 58). Indeed, the principal hegemonic task is "the construction of the very identity of social agents" (*HSS*, p. 58). Hegemony is mistakenly construed as a contingency, even when, as in Gramsci, this contingency becomes the deciding factor of revolutionary strategy. Contingency continues to be inscribed within a logic of necessity and the historically outmoded theory of base and superstructure.

Orthodox Marxism thus fails to adjust to what is, intrinsically, a challenge to its most basic philosophical assumptions. The "crisis of Marxism" is, more precisely, a crisis of *representation*. "The field of politics can no longer be considered a 'representation of interests,' " write Laclau and Mouffe, "given that the so-called 'representation' modifies the nature of what is represented." With the crisis in Marxism, "the very notion of representation as transparency becomes untenable" (*HSS*, p. 58).

The key concept in all this is clearly "articulation": "any relation among elements such that their identity is modified as a result of the articulatory process" (*HSS*, p. 105). In the constant joining, severing, and rejoining of "elements" there subsists, according to Laclau and Mouffe, not merely the untruth of representation and "fixity" but the possibility of an alternative form of praxis. Modernism, even at its most radical, never advances further than this initial negativity. Modernism itself might thus be grasped as a profound movement of "disarticulation" vis-à-vis the apparent refractoriness of the (historical) object. In the light of this thinking, the Adornian aesthetic of negation would be rejected as a half measure—as no more than a kind of negative "essentialism," seeking in the autonomy of the aesthetic a way out of representation that is nevertheless still determined by the "fixity" of certain nondiscursive, extrahegemonic givens.

From the purely formal standpoint of the critique of representation, *Hegemony and Socialist Strategy* would thus seem, through its own grand articulation of linguistic and philosophical elements and strands, to have virtually sidestepped the endlessly troubling difficulties of modernist theory when it seeks to restore immediacy and the possibility of synthesis—vis-à-vis both knowledge and praxis—to something called the "work." For the "work" too entails a "fixity." If representation is, in fact, never more than the movement of articulation, there is no longer any need to abjure the political for the aesthetic. "The path is everything, the goal is nothing."[12] We glimpse, perhaps, a radically distinct notion of the aesthetic itself as emergent in this avoidance of modernist *ressentiment*. Why, if articulation not only denies but affirms, are we obliged to advocate a Beckett over a Brecht—or, for that matter, a Mann over a Kafka?

This line of thinking seems at least worth investigating. But Laclau and Mouffe have, obviously, another agenda. It is not a rethinking of aesthetics but a rethinking of "politics" that *Hegemony and Socialist Strategy* seeks to carry out—not modernism but Marxism that bears here the conservative stigma of representation. From the outset, "articulation" is made to operate not simply as a possible direction in the critique of representation but as itself that which *founds*—the word is unavoidable—the newly de-"essentialized" political theory of "hegemony." Politics is now to be seen as a strictly discursive activity that incessantly creates and re-creates as its own articulatory effects what representational thinking—that is, Marxism—supposes to have been the objectively *given* elements, in the form of classes, means and relations of production, the state, and so forth.

What results from this investment of articulation as a *politically* postmodern locus of agency is, to put it kindly, a philosophical curiosity. Laclau and Mouffe attempt to proceed directly from a poststructuralist critique of the sign that rejects the possibility of any final, fixed meaning not merely to the consequent denial of any fixed system of reference (a patent, though politically unpretentious, retreading of idealism) but to the conclusion that the objective conditions *themselves* can be constructed through a calculated manipulation of the hegemonic *combinatoire*.[13] The "thought/reality" dualism is to be superseded by a monism of "discursive practices" in which a multiplicity of hegemonizing demiurges operates without any necessary constraints. The dialectic of subject and object — still, as we have observed, tenuously retained in the Adornian critique of representation — is thus merely discarded, to be replaced by the "diverse subject positions" already within discourse standing over and against an "exterior . . . constituted by other discourses." (*HSS*, p. 146).

Laclau and Mouffe's strident claims that this discursive reductionism does not in any way entail an abandonment of materialism need not concern us directly here. As Ellen Meiksins Wood has demonstrated vis-à-vis their characterization of the Marx of *Capital* as "economist,"[14] Laclau and Mouffe's purported "materialism" rests on a flagrant and dogmatic misreading of Marxism itself.[15] What is significant here is how, in the effort to claim for articulation a mode of historical and political agency, *Hegemony and Socialist Strategy* must drive itself into a position of radical subjectivism. If there is only articulation, who or what articulates? And if everything is always already articulated, how do we account for change, for the capacity of the system to incorporate new differentiae? This is the problem that has plagued structuralism and poststructuralism since Saussure. Laclau and Mouffe attempt to resolve it by creating new theoretical entities: articulation is, in fact, never total or perfectly "sutured"; it is always "overdetermined." Outside of its structured moments there are always "elements," defined here as the not-yet-fully-articulated. Whence, then, the "elements" if discourse — the space of articulation — fully coats all so-called externals? The answer is that "outside" discourse lies the "field of discursivity": "[T]he exterior is constituted by other discourses" (*HSS*, p. 146). What then is to account for the multiplication of discourses — or to prevent one of these "other discourses" inhabiting the "discursive field" from simply disguising a reintroduction of the transcendental subject?[16]

Laclau and Mouffe's way out of this bind is to ontologize it, to make the problem into its own solution. "It is this ambiguity [that is, the simultaneous impossibility of, and necessity for, "contingency" or a discursive exterior]," they state, "which makes possible articulation as a practice instituting nodal points which partially fix the meaning of the social in an organized system of differences" (*HSS*, p. 134). This "relational space unable to constitute itself as such" is simply given a name, "society," which sanctions the theoretical impasse in one fell swoop (*HSS*, p. 113). "Society" in effect becomes the alias for an absolute and transcendental subject. Laclau concedes as much in a more recent article: "If . . . there is no ultimate ground, political argument increases in importance, for it constructs social reality. Society can then be understood as a vast argumentative texture in which humankind constructs its own reality."[17]

Critical analysis of both paralogy and hegemony/articulation would, then, suggest that behind postmodernism's ethico-political change of skin there occurs a movement to supplant the objective idealism of an Adorno with a stance (admittedly somewhat heterodoxical) of subjective idealism. The effect of the postmodernist rethinking of representation and the crisis implicated in its breakdown as the constituent philosopheme of history and society becomes the annulment of crisis itself as a reality grounded in an objective historical development.

Again we must recall that in the Adornian formulation the crisis in representation obeys a historical logic. Representation no longer works because the historical object itself—whether fascism, culture industry, or administered universe—exceeds in its inherent abstraction the limits of any socially based cognition or revolutionary agency. Modernism as ideology represents the incapacity to think this abstraction—the relations inscribed in capital—as precisely a material outcome of historical development. History, including its subjective aspect, becomes a function of a preordained abstraction, rather than the inverse.

In the postmodern thinking of representational crisis as I read it, this quality of nonidentity or noncorrespondence is no longer sought in the object, whether as real or ideal abstraction, but *in the subject*, albeit here construed as a discursive category without ontological foundation. Representation fails to work—the adverb ''no longer'' ceases to be apposite—not because the object rules out any positive identification by the subject but because ''fixity'' per se, independent of any object, has been rendered problematic. The movement away from aesthetics and toward ''politics'' is here simply the result of conferring upon the subject the illusory freedom of motion that a complete break with objectivity allows as one of its side effects.

In effect, then, postmodernism simply severs the agency of the ''work'' from its negative determination in the nonrepresentable historical object, so that it becomes, in the phraseology of deconstruction, a ''floating signifier.'' Laclau and Mouffe maneuver this cypher into the language of a ''radical democratic'' politics; Lyotard into the more modest language of speech-act theory. But these are the free options of epistemological nihilism. We can, if we want, do even better than Adorno in the cultivation of the dismal—witness the postmodernism of Jean Baudrillard.[18] In the end, postmodernism's promise of subversion, if it should choose to make one, seems no more and no less genuine than that long-ago discredited pledge of the modernist vanguard to, as it were, seize hold of capital's cultural and psychic mechanisms without firing a shot.

3

A critique of ideology, however, implies some access to a nonideological, scientific path—a line of criticism that can stand inverted thinking back on its feet.

Given that, with the inception of modern capitalism itself, the broadly signifying categories of representation and historical agency do confront critical thinking as problematic, do undergo a "crisis," where, then, is this critical-scientific path to be sought?

It is this question that leads us, via Adorno, to the *Eighteenth Brumaire* and to my own complexly motivated reading of that text in Chapter 1. Enjoying the advantages of a postmodern hindsight, I shall limit myself here to an abstract and partial summary of its results, which, it should be cautioned, is no substitute for the process of "reading" as such.

What we find in the *Brumaire* are the rough, tenuously theoretical outlines of a *dialectical* critique of representation. Marx's central problem, of course, is not representation per se but the state: specifically, how to account for the existence of a bourgeois dictatorship that also, in certain flagrant instances, acts in contradiction to the perceived interests of the bourgeoisie itself. Does this not, in fact, contradict the theory of state power as an institutional representation of the interests of the ruling class? Marx's solution to this apparent enigma is to point to what appears to be a historically evolved disjuncture between bourgeois "interest," as it is perceived and defended by private bourgeois individuals, and something he calls the "material power" (*materielle Macht*) of the class as a whole. It is this "material power" that the dictatorship of Louis Bonaparte represents — in essence, the more fully unfolded, real abstraction of *capital* itself, as Marx was subsequently to understand it in a more consciously theoretical mode in the *Grundrisse* and *Capital*. The "interests" of capital as such are here perceived as not fully identical with the "interests" of the class — *itself* in a state of transformation — which monopolizes it as something "private."

The state, then, represents the bourgeoisie and yet does not. Capital represents the private ownership of the means of production and yet, at the same time, something that already exceeds this particular mode of privatization. The *Brumaire* makes no explicit attempt to solve this riddle. But the only conclusion to be drawn from this, vis-à-vis representation and consistent with Marx's general method, is that a relation of nonidentity enters into force — a nonidentity, however, that is itself not absolute but relative, mediated. Representation "works," but only provisionally, only as approximation. The identity of representative and represented is strictly a postulate; though it can never be fully realized, it is nevertheless required in any scientific, objectively valid thinking process. It is this dialectical practice of representation that Marx indirectly sets forth in the splendid passage contrasting the "revolutions of the eighteenth century" and those of the nineteenth, the "social revolution."[19] The former are characterized precisely by their apparent surplus of representational identity, which, however, is quickly transformed into mere fiction, a representational falsehood. The latter encounter representation as always deficient, always only an approximation that must be continually discarded and replaced. "Then the words went beyond the content, now the content goes beyond the words."

It goes without saying that such a dialectical practice of representation presupposes a dialectical materialism—that is, the epistemological standpoint that grasps the external as *both* real *and* governed by a continual movement of nonidentity, or contradiction. Lacking this standpoint, representation must indeed strike the inhabitant of modern capitalist society as irredeemably false, as the postulate of an ideal identity that the "opacity of the social" inevitably undermines. To hold, *in the absence of a materialist dialectic*, to a positive belief in representation as simple transparence is most surely to fall into "essentialism."

And it is, not coincidentally, just this "essentialism" that acts as both the lost origin and the implicit utopian horizon for modernists like Adorno and postmodernists like Laclau and Mouffe. This is readily seen, for example, when the authors of *Hegemony and Socialist Strategy* attack the "authoritarian," "representational" politics of Leninism for its allegiance to a principle of "historical class interests" as "against" the "real working class." (*HSS*, p. 59). The nonidentity between the "historical interests" of the proletariat and the "real working class" is here posed as absolute, *fixed*. According to Wood, "What [this] effectively means is that, where there is no simple, absolute, mechanical, unilinear and noncontradictory determination, there is no determinacy, no relationship, no causality at all."[20] What is this if not the *political essentialism* that Laclau and Mouffe so assiduously seek to avoid?

In flight from the essentialism that it covertly desires and inadvertently evokes in its defensive gestures, postmodernism à la Laclau and Mouffe seeks "unfixity" but can attribute it only to the hypersubjective pole of "discourse" and "articulation." Perhaps this qualifies as the uniquely postmodern inversion: unequipped to think *reality* as a continual movement through identity to nonidentity, as "unfixity," postmodernism simply discards it as no more than the "effect" of an unfixity occupying the site of the transcendental subject. Here, as throughout, the dialectical standpoint is excluded. It is with unquestionable acumen that Wood speaks, in this context, of a "Platonic Marxism."[21]

II

1

In *Modernism and Hegemony* I advance the theory that the ideology of modernism must be grasped as coeval, in its genesis, with the modern discourse of aesthetics per se—that in the aestheticizing of the crisis in representation and historical agency, the crucial ideological inversion already completes itself. In the appeal to the agency of the "work" there is an ideologically implicit reference to capital (the social abstraction) as a species of secular black hole into which all

representationally mediated activity has been collapsed. It is the (real, historically determined) "self-activity" of capital in the progression from its primitive
to its modern forms as industrial and monopoly-finance capital that inverts itself
in the seemingly concrete, but historically indeterminate, agency of the autonomous artwork.

There is, however, assumed in this theoretical configuration a certain structural integrity, both a sequential ordering and a definite, unified terrain, such that
the *cause*—capital in its abstract self-movement—is directly present in its
effects—the breakdown of traditional representational bonds of identity leading
to a generalized sense of "crisis." Modernism can emerge as the impulse to constitute a nonabstract locus of agency that at the same time escapes the collapse of
representation—the modern formula for aesthetics—only insofar as the unfolding of the social abstraction is equally and progressively felt in all superstructural
spheres. In order to be sensed as the final destruction of all qualitative identity—
as the real, social abstraction—capital must already have become the universal
ground of sensation: this is the logic that becomes the conscious point of departure for the Adornian aesthetic philosophy, which then sets itself the problematic
task of locating a standpoint of negativity that transcends the ground at the same
time that it acknowledges its universality. Hence, the ultimately paradoxical locus of the "work" as an exclusionary ground—as the ground reserved only for
itself: "Art is the social antithesis of society."[22] The theory of capital, or of social abstraction, as the universal ground of all activity, although retaining a certain limited formal truth, leads, as I seek to argue in the conclusion of Chapter 1,
to the characteristically modernist inversion whereby capital comes to embody
the historical dialectic only in order to terminate it. But it may also be observed
that such a theory is limited not only by its own propensity for idealistic inversion
but by its very logic of history—or its end—as posed upon a uniform terrain.
There would appear to be no space in this thinking—and this applies particularly
to Adorno—for the process referred to by dialecticians as "uneven" or "unequal
development." Must the historical unfolding of autonomous capital proceed
evenly within the parameters of a universal ground? High modernism, if it could
pose the question at all, would answer affirmatively.

But to deny uneven development, even if only for purposes of theoretical construction, is to deny history yet again. "Universal history is always the history of
unequal development."[23] The freeing of capital from the representational fixa-
tions that reflected its primitive forms of emergence does not lead directly to
its universal grounding of all societal transactions, even if it produces a definite
convergence in the direction of such a grounding as an abstract limit.[24] Readily
concealed from the metropolitan perspective of the world surveyed, whether will-
ingly or reluctantly, through the eyes of capital at its pinnacle of abstract self-
containment, the reality of unevenness is unavoidably exposed at the periphery,
that is, those social and historical loci where capital concentrates its most ex-

treme contradictions. Here the modern and its Other meet along a boundary more spatial than temporal; representation does not "break down" in the wake of "inhuman" abstraction but might be said, rather, to become distended over the ruptural divide between capital as *ratio* and the flagrant "irrationalities" that it erects along its path. "All that is solid melts into air" — and yet, at the perimeter of its dissolving stain, capital precipitates and pushes to its margins a great mass of unused and explosive solids. There is, to use Andre Gunder Frank's precise phrase, "development of underdevelopment." Its living emblem is the great, modern metropolis of the Third World — a Mexico City, São Paulo, or Manila — with its towering commercial and financial strongholds enclosed within a massive ring of pillaged human beings living within sight of modernity but yet beneath its plane.

Speaking highly abstractly, can we not now assert that under such conditions the crisis in representation is overshadowed and displaced by the crisis of the ground itself as the terrain upon which the unity of the historical subject with its object is both affirmed *and* denied? Representation does not, as a consequence, lose its problematic aspect. But the dialectic stipulating its falsity and the necessity to overcome it in a "work" that directly contains an otherwise impossible synthesis gives way to the more urgent project of producing the terrain of synthesis per se. The "work" can appear to make available the ideological space for this synthesis only insofar as there can be conferred upon it a property of negative correspondence to a social abstraction — capital — that has become the real space of synthesis, even if it is an empty space. But insofar as this real space itself is sundered, insofar as the law of progressive abstraction collides with its own reality as "development of underdevelopment," must not the agency of the "work" as a negative closure become suspended by the more pressing drive to *mediate* the split dividing both historical subject and historical object along the transverse axis of their ground?

And is it not then this suspension, or even overdetermination, of the "work" understood as a locus of negation drawn against a plane of unrepresentable abstraction — a suspension *within* the space of a purely mediatory agency lodged between two apparently incommensurable realities — that must foreground any critical approach to modernism at the periphery? The third and fourth essays of *Modernism and Hegemony* can be read as an initial effort to deepen and flesh out such a thesis with respect to modernist developments in two Latin-American societies, Mexico and Brazil. Again, as with the Adorno fragment and the *Eighteenth Brumaire*, my initial selection of texts has not been consciously governed by the need to corroborate this thesis, stated here in its abstract generality. Critical discussions of texts by Juan Rulfo, Octavio Paz, Oswald de Andrade, Joaquim Pedro de Andrade, Roberto Schwarz, Glauber Rocha, and others represent a perhaps somewhat fortuitous constellation of reference points for an originally intuitive and nonsystematic sense of the problem.

Less arbitrary here, perhaps, are the distinct but analagous theoretical "meta-narratives" of the work as mediatory agency that both inform and derive from Rulfian and Oswaldian textual practices. Following Angel Rama (and, through him, Fernando Ortiz), I have invoked the formula of "transculturation" to typify those practices.[25] Briefly summarized, "transculturation" describes the mediatory agency whereby the Latin-American work of art actively transforms and regrounds the modernism of the metropolis by prompting a synthesis of the metropolis's antirationalism with the prerationalization of rural peasant and indigenous tribal cultures. "Magical realism" is another, less precise, name for this procedure. "Consumptive production," as the central theoretical topic of Chapter 4, represents a would-be Marxian amplification of Oswald's seminal cultural slogan of *antropofagia* and refers here to the more economically nuanced mediation in which *consumption* of the imported culture, practiced as a kind of carnivalized expropriation of alien civilization, becomes itself the constituting moment of a unified peripheral subject.

The reader may refer directly to Chapter 3 and 4 for a fuller account of these two "peripheral" modernisms. What I wish to set forth here, partly by way of a self-critical emendation, is that both transculturation and consumptive production entail somewhat more than simply the theory of the work as mediating agency. The impetus to mediate, to reground a distended or even sundered historical identity, is, after all, scarcely the unique property of the avant-garde in Latin America. It is, in fact, a dominant theme of Latin-American ideology since at least the period of independence and the rise of the creole bourgeoisies. The question is, Who, or what, is to mediate whom? The notorious slogans of nineteenth-century "enlighteners" left no doubt on this score. *Civilización* remains the standard of measure, even if its impossibility as ground is acknowledged. What particularly distinguishes the modernist (not necessarily *modernista*) variation on this theme is the logic of an inverse, or *counter*mediation. Both transculturation and consumptive production describe a process in which it is *barbarie* that poses itself as the actively mediating agent. It becomes the task of the work—in strict alliance with the sphere of subaltern cultural practices rather than in rebellious refusal of all established culture per se—to anticipate and project this inversion on the level of its own artistic structure. In this way the work itself becomes the imaginary equivalent, rather than simply the allegorizing representation, of the unified ground upon which the subject and object of local history can meet face-to-face.

What, it must then be asked, determines this reversal of the mediational polarity of the work? What is it about the transcultural or anthropophagous work that enables it, as it were, to colonize the colonizer? Modernism can here point to the increased role of the Latin-American "barbarous" masses themselves in assessing and contesting their "civilizing" mediations and mediators. And indeed, that an incipiently democratic energy furnishes the impulse toward a modernism attuned to the realities of uneven development is a fact it would be pointless to deny. But is it warranted to assume that the terms of the countermediation as worked out in the textual configurations of the *real maravilloso* and *antropofagia* are no more than the direct expression of this democratic impulse? The fact that the modernism of Rulfo and Oswald rides the crest of what is clearly more than just an intellectual and petit bourgeois revolt may equally denote a movement to redirect and contain this (in itself contradictory) movement.

It is this latter capacity of countermediation to act as itself a "strategy of containment" that Chapter 3 and Chapter 4 purport to explore. And it is here that the concept of hegemony derives its importance in relation to my general argument. Concisely stated, my exploratory critique of "peripheral" modernism proposes that, in formulating what appears to be an artistically immanent solution to the crisis of the ground, modernist textual practices in fact respond to the need to reimage and restructure the problem of a peripheral capitalist hegemony itself. The problem of the ground, and its suspension of the more typically metropolitan problem of representation, becomes in my view an ideological abstraction of the basic historical problems of capitalist rule itself, in both the Latin-American and the overall imperialist periphery. What determines the general shift to a modernist aesthetic of countermediation is, I argue, on the one hand, the enhanced power and rationalization of the peripheral bourgeois state itself—typically as a result of populist revolutions or coups led by the middle class—and, on the other, the fact that this same rationalization only elevates to a higher plane the contradiction between itself and the prevailing political "irrationality," that is, the relative absence of political subjects able or willing to act as the "molecular" units of peripheral capitalist rule. The transcultural or anthropophagous work both reflects and imaginatively "solves" this contradiction by constructing the "space" of this missing hegemony as if it were purely the outgrowth of an autochthonous cultural substance or activity. The social abstraction—embodied and concentrated here in the state—seeks to reduce the identity of its Other to the status of one of its mediations. But by the very fact that the state's own development continuously reproduces this Other even as it incorporates it, such mediation must appear to reverse itself, must take the form of a cultural surrogate for hegemony rather than a hegemonic culture.

2

The critical line I have attempted to pursue here with respect to the theory and practice of art as countermediational must be acknowledged as reflecting in part an overall trend within recent Latin-American criticism and theory, in which the preeminent concern for Otherness—alterity—as a locus of *mediation* accedes to an approach to alterity as ultimately unmediated and "for itself." My brief, and no doubt less than satisfactory allusions to Traven's *The Cotton Pickers* and to the "aesthetic of hunger" films of Brazilian Cinema Novo's middle period as the

possible indices of a peripheral aesthetic that looks beyond the hegemonic interests of the national bourgeoisies—as potential models for a revolutionary, postpopulist art no longer encumbered by cultural nationalism—stem from an increasingly shared sense of skepticism toward any goal of synthesis in which
class, gender, and ethnic differences are finally suspended in some nationalist or
regionalist pact with oppressive totality.

Looking at artistic developments in Latin America since the "boom," however, we can take note of an emergent form that perhaps lays the strongest claim
to expressing in directly narrative terms this rethinking of alterity. I refer here, of
course, to "testimonial" writing, including the so-called testimonial novel. Beginning with Miguel Barnet's *Biografía de un cimarrón* (1967) and extending
into the 1970s and 1980s with such widely read texts as Omar Cabezas's *La montaña es algo más que una inmensa estepa verde* (1982) and *Me llamo Rigoberta
Menchú y así me nació la consciencia* (1983), the testimonial narrative has by
now perhaps passed its zenith; but an unmistakably "testimonial" aesthetic continues to influence contemporary Latin-American writing profoundly. I could cite
as examples here the recent novels of the Salvadoran writer Manlio Argueta or
Eduardo Galeano's epic trilogy of quasi-testimonial vignettes.[26]

Much of the interest in the testimonial, which now extends to certain metropolitan circles, undoubtedly stems from its obvious links to the intensified class
struggles in the Southern Cone of the 1970s and the Central America of the
1980s. However, we must note that in addition to this topicality, there is in the
reception of the testimonial a strong disposition to read it as a more direct narrative conveyance of the Other in its social and historical immediacy. Here the fictional impersonations of the quasi-populist "boom" text are dropped—alterity
becomes the end rather than the means of a postcolonial aesthetic. Of course, the
mediations of the editor/ethnologist demonstrate this literal directness to be a
myth; but the basic impulse to restore to the Other what now appears to be its
inherent truth may be felt to inform even this partial screen. Thus, for example,
Miguel Barnet is able to write that the heroes of his first two testimonial novels
"are, without meaning to be, real witnesses, in sociological rather than literary
terms, because, despite the fact that they are re-created by me, manipulated by
means of certain fictional strands, they are beings of flesh and blood, real and
convincing."[27] What we typically find linked to this tendency for an ethnographic and autobiographical portrayal of alterity is an intellectual gravitation toward the realm of factual immediacy and the "everyday" (*lo cotidiano*) as the
authentic medium of alterity. Even a quasi-epical narrative such as Cabezas's *La
montaña* emphasizes almost to exclusion the quotidian aspect of clandestinity
and guerrilla warfare. That this antiheroic posture stems in crucial ways from a
left reaction against the excessive and tragic messianism of the *foco* is a factor not
to be overlooked. But the very fact that a popular-cultural immediacy becomes
linked, in the testimonial aesthetic, to an alterity "for itself" and without medi-

ation may tempt us to detect here a certain affinity for the postmodern. To evoke this term with respect to the testimonial narrative may seem outwardly obtuse — evidently we have here to do with two very disparate types of "surfaces." Still, the philosophical and theoretical realignments that appear to underpin and accompany the testimonial aesthetic cannot help but seem oddly familiar, if also exotic, in light of contemporary metropolitan intellectual vanguards. The turn from alterity as a formal means serving an aesthetics of countermediation to alterity as a kind of absolute, irreducible content, like the metropolitan postmodern turn discussed above, shows a peculiar tendency to contradict its (arguably) radical political impulse with a distinctly right-wing epistemology.

To demonstrate this with respect to the testimonial would require a fairly extensive critique centering on what, to my thinking, stands out as it most damaging contradiction—its tendency to fetishize the immediate and quotidian plane of history in a manner suggesting a reversion to naturalism. That the Other, particulary when female and/or nonwhite, has traditionally been relegated to this domestic, subepical dimension by the master narratives of imperialism and peripheral nationalism alike may, indeed, explain why a kind of naturalizing inflection or tactic becomes necessary in the effort to portray new historical subjects. But even in testimonial-like narratives such as Argueta's *Un día de vida*, in which there is an attempt made to rejoin this ethnographic, domestic poetics with the epical narrative of the Salvadoran civil war, the "survival ethic"[28] inherited from the testimonial often drowns out the specific historical and political essences of characters and events.

But to draw out these contradictions in recent Latin-American thought in a more succinct manner, it is necessary to turn to certain openly theoretical and philosophical formulations of postmodern alterity. I have chosen for this purpose the philosophical work of Enrique Dussel, an Argentine theologian and church historian strongly linked with the liberation theology movement. It is to his *Filosofía de la liberación*[29] that I now briefly turn.

Dussel's *Philosophy of Liberation* is, of course, neither the first nor the most complete attempt to propound philosophically the standpoint of alterity. Much of what Dussel writes takes its conscious point of departure from the work of European phenomenology, existentialism, and poststructuralism; the philosophy of Eugene Levinas clearly stands out among these as a major influence. The unique feature here is that Dussel attempts to assign to the Other not merely a logical but a fully *spatial* being.

> Space as a battlefield, as a geography studied to destroy an enemy, as a territory with fixed frontiers, is very different from the abstract idealization of empty space of Newton's physics or the existential space of phenomenology. Abstract spaces are naive, nonconflictual unrealities. The space of a world within the ontological horizon is the space of a

world center, of the organic, self-conscious state that brooks no contradictions—because it is an imperialist state. (*PL*, p. 1)

The primordial division of space, its fundamental noncontiguity—that which I have characterized as the crisis of the ground—becomes, for Dussel, the basis on which to rethink the entire history of philosophy. Classical Western philosophy, understood preeminently as ontology, is here *already* the thinking of a geographic center engaged in the subjugation of a periphery. "Before the *ego cogito* there is an *ego conquiro*; 'I conquer' is the practical foundation of 'I think' " (*PL*, p. 30). "Classic philosophy of all ages is the theoretical consummation of the practical oppression of the peripheries" (*PL*, p. 5).

A philosophy of liberation for Latin America—and the periphery—must, therefore, set forth from a refusal of all ontology. "Our thought sets out from non-Being, nothingness, otherness, exteriority, the mystery of no-sense" (*PL*, p. 14). The periphery itself, moreover, becomes the only ground upon which a genuine philosophy of liberation can arise. "Distant thinkers, those who had a perspective of the center from the periphery . . . , these are the ones who have a clear mind for pondering reality"(*PL*, p. 4). Although certain "post-Hegelian critics of the European left" may have begun the theoretical task of unmasking ontological imperialism, "only the praxis of oppressed peoples of the periphery, of the woman violated by masculine ideology, of the subjugated child, can fully reveal it to us" (*PL*, p. 15).

Not surprisingly, the refusal of 'ontology" leads Dussel in the direction of a Husserlian phenomenology. But the postulation of alterity as a "nonbeing" that does not thereby submit to the bracketing of its real existence—as a "reality beyond being"—clearly requires going beyond the phenomenological method. But a going beyond in what direction?

It is here that *Philosophy of Liberation* confronts what is effectively its chief contestant with respect to the openly historical and political claims that Dussel makes for alterity as both agency and cognitive ground. This is, of course, the method of dialectics. Like the metropolitan postmodernists, Dussel equates the dialectical method with its Hegelian formulation. That is, for Dussel the dialectic is essentially a philosophy of movement toward a final and arrested identity. "[D]ialectic goes through [*dia*] various ontic horizons from totality . . . to totality until it arrives at the fundamental one. . . . It does not demonstrate the foundation; but shows . . . its final coherence in the identity of the system as totality in which all differences . . . recover their ultimate meaning" (*PL*, pp. 157–58).[30]

Thus it is foundationalism—a positing of the self-identical ground of all difference—that finally vitiates dialectics as a method and philosophy of liberation. Dussel concurs here with Laclau and the metropolitan postmodernists. Hegel becomes, in *Philosophy of Liberation*, the supreme representative of a classical ontology expressing, through its final inclusion of all exteriority within the sameness of being, the annihilation of the Other.[31]

But *Philosophy of Liberation* makes what looks like a key departure here. For Dussel, the Other—that which is finally exterior to any total system of structured differences, beyond and outside foundations—is not simply to be affirmed in its abstract formality but is, rather, openly identified with the oppressed subjects of the periphery. The problem of identifying a subject of paralogy, or of hegemony, which leads Lyotard and Laclau and Mouffe into logical aporias, seems to find a concrete and practical resolution in Dussel's explicit identification of this subject with a peripheral—that is, a practically and not merely theoretically decentered—locus of alterity. Dussel thus appears to discover a concrete, historical subject to correspond to the ideal postulate of a postmodern agency.

But it is already too late for this maneuver. And Dussel, as it happens, remains consistent enough with his own standards of thinking to proclaim openly the fact that this absolute Other, this transontological exteriority that he attributes to the oppressed masses of the periphery, must in the final analysis be conceded to be a purely metaphysical agency. Thus, under the subheading of "The Being Which Is Not Merely Being," Dussel writes:

> Exteriority, which does not have the same meaning as it did for Hegel [,] . . . is meant to signify the ambit whence other persons, as free and not conditioned by one's own system and not as part of one's own world, reveal themselves.

And a few paragraphs below this:

> Only the free person, each person, is the self-substantive, autonomous, other totality: metaphysical exteriority, the most real reality beyond the world of Being. (*PL*, pp. 40–41)

It is then only a brief step from this "other person," who is "properly real, more real that the cosmic totality," to God the Creator (*PL*, p. 41). In line with his espousal of the "Semitic" tradition in religious thought, Dussel invokes the Machabees and their God as "absolute Other," who "created all out of non-Being." "The metaphysical theory of creation," argues *The Philosophy of Liberation*:

> is the theoretical support of liberative revolution; it is the most thorough-going deposition that no system is eternal, because everything, even the sun and the earth, is contingent (it could be nonexistent) and possible, nonnecessary (at a given time it was not). (*PL*, p. 100)

Here we do not find the calculated evasions concealed in last-minute appeals to "overdetermination" and the contingent as "other discourses." "New systems," we are openly told, "come from nothingness" (*PL*, p. 45). "What reason can never embrace—the mystery of the other as other—only faith can penetrate'' (*PL*, p. 46).

It may be objected here that *Philosophy of Liberation* strays from the path of postmodern theory when it "substantializes," so to speak, the principle of alterity, or "unfixity," that for metropolitan postmodernism remains strictly an attribute of relationality. But the truth, I would argue, is just the opposite: Dussel follows the path to its metaphysical end point. What other manner of agency can there be for a thinking that abjures all principles of historical or social determinacy as "essentialist"?

This self-consistency on Dussel's part is further reflected in his freely proclaiming a *method* appropriate to the metaphysics that he opposes to all philosophies of being. This he dubs the "analectic," as against the dialectic, method. While granting to the latter its "moment" as the movement of thought toward an ever more inclusive totality, the analectic moment "opens us up to the metaphysical sphere . . . referring us to the other"(*PL*, p. 159).

> In the final analysis it can be affirmed that the analectic moment of dialectics is founded on the absolute anteriority of exteriority over totality, even to affirming the priority of the Absolute Other as creative origin over creation as work, as a finite and therefore perfectible totality. (*PL*, p. 192)

Though outwardly shorn of its metaphysical entailments, the method of "exteriority over totality" has arguably come to characterize an important current of contemporary thinking on and in Latin America. This is particularly true of works by metropolitan writers within the ambit of poststructuralism and deconstruction. Todorov's *Conquest of America* may be cited as a prime example. But explicitly poststructuralist affinities are no prerequisite here. I will be the first to concede that *Modernism and Hegemony*, in its approach to the question of Latin America and its "alterity," is not entirely free of "analectics."

In fact, what is probably the classic application of the analectic to Latin-American literary and cultural theory appears in two widely read essays written by the Cuban author and critic Roberto Fernández Retamar, "Para una teoría de la literatura hispanoamericana" (1972/1975) and "Algunas problemas teóricas de la literatura hispanoamericana" (1974).[32] Here Retamar seeks to refute the assumption that "universal" theories of literature formulated in *euronorteamérica* can be directly applied to Latin-American (or Hispanic American) literary practice. This is argued not merely because such theories—epitomized for Retamar in the stylistics of René Wellek and in Western structuralism—imperiously assimilate to a metropolitan standard a peripheral reality misconstrued or ignored by the metropolis; it is rather because the underlying concept of totality—Goethe's *Weltliteratur*—itself has no reality. "The one world does not exist"; but "a

Hispano-American Literature exists,'' insists Retamar, ''because Hispano-America exists.''[33]

Such a standpoint, as was subsequently argued by Retamar's disciple Deside-rio Navarro, ultimately leads either to an empiricist *reductio* or to a purely reac-tive posture of regional solipsism.[34] Navarro himself attempts to guide the cri-tique of Eurocentrist theory out of this impasse by advocating a ''comparative study'' of the various regional and national literatures that respects their partial autonomy while remaining faithful to the scientific imperative of generalizing the knowledge of their specific variations. That is, Navarro simply advocates an eclecticism. Against both we can easily imagine a more orthodoxly postmodern theory—following, perhaps, Deleuze and Guattari's notion of a ''minor'' literature—whereby the ''region'' itself is reaffirmed as purely a mark of un-fixed, limitless alterity. In the end, however, each of these approaches to the question of literary alterity inverts the crisis of the ground such that rupture and unevenness are no longer grasped as the products of a given historical development—that of the present capitalist world market and division of labor—but become primordial realities that are simply masked by universalistic fictions. The Other becomes a strange sort of entity that, although making its appearance in history, no sooner appears than it retracts its being onto a plane of abstract spatiality. Reading Retamar and Navarro, we are led to conclude that the same historical forces that produced ''Nuestra América,'' having now produced it, come to an abrupt halt, so that one speaks of the product itself—or the multiplic-ity of these, since other regions are also deemed to exist—as something quite independent. Despite having emerged from the same crucible of historical con-tingency, the identical world-historical ground, center and periphery enter into relations of absolute exteriority.

All that prevents such a critique of Eurocentrism from becoming the perfect model of Dussel's analectic method is its failure to posit outright the presence of a metaphysical agency. But, unfriendly as Retamar, Navarro, and others who fol-low in this particular ''postmodern'' groove would undoubtedly be to the idea, the theoretical entity they variously construct under the sign of the Other—that which makes its appearance in History while remaining somehow outside and beyond it—harmonizes remarkably well with the Christian concept of a divine redeemer. Understanding this, Dussel takes full advantage of it. For if, as the ''philosophy of liberation'' asserts, imperialism is written into all philosophies of the world as united in its objective being—so that, as the inverted reasoning goes, it is the thinking of imperialism that determines its concrete historical and social being[35]—what but an otherwordly thinking can successfully lead us on the path of emancipation? The principle of exteriority as anterior to totality, if it is not to remain a merely conceptual hypostasis, must, as Dussel quite logically concludes, entail a metaphysical totality. ''The metaphysics of creation is the ul-timate foundation [Grund] of political, historical liberation'' (*PL*, p. 92).

That is, from absolute Otherness, we arrive in the end at the absolute sameness of divine substance. To the contingent fetishisms of imperialism there is counterposed the supreme fetish—"uneven development," freed not of unevenness but of development in general. Made over into the hypostatic origin of analectics, the Other, like Laclau and Mouffe's unfixity, simply produces its opposite. The "going beyond" the dialectical method promised here by Dussel's postmodern philosophy of liberation thus falls back behind the dialectical point of departure which "grasps these opposites not as dead, rigid, but as living, conditional, mobile, becoming transformed into one another."[36]

III

In the course of both outlining and criticizing what have seemed to me to represent significant but unsuccessful attempts to rectify the ideological inversions of modernist theory, I have perhaps failed to pose, much less answer, the ultimately crucial question: namely, What new historical developments in the spheres of politics and economics act to determine the ideological shifts evident in postmodernism? The relative paucity of Marxist attempts to grapple with this question enforces something of a silence on my part, since the kind of detailed analysis of contemporary class struggles that would have to support any warrantable conclusions in this respect exceeds the limits of this work. One well-known exception on this score is the recent work of Fredric Jameson, in which there is a broad attempt made to interpret the postmodern as a unified aesthetic proper to late, multinational capitalism.[37] Jameson's work has received much attention and much criticism, which I do not now wish to broach. However, the fact that I have taken the approach of framing both modernism and postmodernism as theoretical and even quasi-political discourses—as more in the nature, to use Lyotard's term, of "metanarratives" than of transparent, self-contained "aesthetics"—makes the Jamesonian route toward periodization problematic for my purposes. What I shall permit myself to suggest here, by way of conclusion, should therefore be taken simply as a thinking out loud in the absence of the necessary critical and scientific spadework.

In the preface to *Intellectual and Manual Labour*, Alfred Sohn-Rethel remarks of the "Western" Marxism of Lukács, Benjamin, Adorno and others that its often exclusive fixation on superstructures reflects "the revolution that never happened."[38] The reference here is to the failed Central European revolutions of 1918–1919, but clearly this "absent" revolution vis-à-vis the metropolitan West extends to the temporary victory of fascism and the eventual failure of revolutionaries to turn its military defeat into an overthrow of its capitalist basis. As I see them, however, the intellectual and cultural ramifications of this defeat— partially analyzed by Perry Anderson[39]—extend beyond the boundaries of a "Western" Marxism per se to include what I seek to characterize as the ideology of modernism. The problem of agency as it enters the theoretical discourses of modernists such as Adorno is a problem essentially bequeathed by this historical, political defeat and the complex weave of factors leading to its denouement. Despite what is sometimes a conscious awareness of this epochal ground, however, the characteristic tendency across the intellectual and cultural spectrum of the Western avant-garde is to separate the question of agency from the historical circumstances that have directly contributed to pose it.

With the 1960s, however, as variously periodized by a host of cultural critics both right and left, there seems to take place a major political reawakening throughout much of the world. And perhaps it can now be generally agreed that it is the repoliticized, resurgent class struggle of this period that lays the basis for what is subsequently labeled the postmodern. The sixties effectively challenge the received, modernist notions of the avant-garde, both cultural and political, at the core as also at the periphery. An array of newly mobilized and radicalized "subjects" explodes upon the scene. Such, at least, is the popular conception.

A correct and profound criticism of postmodernism will hinge, however, on how we *assess the outcome* of these politically and culturally decisive struggles. Do the sixties permit us to speak of a genuinely restored and transformed revolutionary agency, prepared, in ways unsuspected by the traditional vanguards, to set aside the "dialectic of defeat"?

Such, it would seem, is the dogma of a *Hegemony and Socialist Strategy*, as likewise of a *Philosophy of Liberation*. A more dystopian postmodernism—with Baudrillard at its theoretical center—would, ostensibly of course, balk at even these scrupulously de-classed manifestos, reading them, perhaps, as no more than the "simulated" radicalisms generated by a now fully cybernized and protean culture industry. But, to those attempting to hold to and advance a dialectical grasp of the present in light of the recent surge and apparently subsequent quiescence (at least outside the periphery) of class struggles, there can be no meaningful distinction here. The "lessons of the sixties" are, I believe, neither so serendipitous nor so apocalyptic.

It must, at the outset, be clearly stipulated that crucial political advances resulted from the radical social movements that swept much of the world two decades ago. The resurfacing and growth of a class-conscious feminism and anti-racism represent a genuinely historic victory that the present counterrevolutionary resurgence has been unable to reverse. That the maintenance of modern monopoly and state capitalism rests in an intrinsic way on the "special" oppression and superexploitation of women and nonwhites is a truth the consequences of which no serious radical politics can reasonably set aside.

But the fundamental problem—that which a theoretical consciousness encounters in the category of agency—remains historically unresolved. There persists a crisis in agency, reflecting itself in, among other things, a crisis in Marxism. For despite the real advances, the struggles of the sixties failed to overcome effectively the fundamental political contradictions and errors that led to Sohn-Rethel's "revolution that never happened" and that, in the decades following, have restored the rule of essentially capitalist elites in the once proletarian-governed East. The event known to the West as China's Cultural Revolution represents, in this global context, the really signal moment here—both in its clear-sighted objective of ousting China's "red bourgeoisie" and in its ultimate failure as a result of its own ideological confusion regarding the complex identity of its opponent.

I am conscious, of course, of the highly polemicized ground upon which I tread here, and beg the reader's inindulgence toward my perhaps reckless allusions to questions that in the general course of critical debates remain safely bracketed. But it is to these issues that the crisis in agency necessarily beckons us, if we are to avoid the modernist and postmodernist route to plain idealism and metaphysics. Simply to read into the sixties, as is now customary, an emergence of new modes of historical agency that point the way around the current setbacks and confusions of Marxist-led class struggles is itself to indulge in a provincial and elitist utopianism, often as not guided by theoretical throwbacks to pragmatism and theology. The latest developments in so-called New Left thought reflect, on the whole, the seemingly permanent incapacity of this movement to carry out anything more than a superficial and tendentially pre-Marxist critique of its "Old" precursor. In this sense it is still the Old Left and not a genuine New Left that emerges as the ironic victor in the course of the last two decades.[40] Meanwhile, the turn toward a neo-populist, quasi-anarchist, and often expressly metaphysical politics of marginality and the "quotidian" in Latin America, though it undoubtedly reflects a basic tactical necessity in the immediate wake of the temporary victories of imperialist counterinsurgency, becomes, once it is elevated to the status of a new revolutionary theory, a similarly fruitless exercise in postmodernist utopianism.

The fundamental problems of theory and strategy confronting us—problems posed by the reversal of the socialism heroically carved out by the Old Left—must, as Sohn-Rethel has expressed it, lead "deeper into Marxism" and not into retooled versions of Heidegger, Wittgenstein, and William James. And if they lead us to any texts at all, one such text is the *Eighteenth Brumaire*.

Modernism and Hegemony

Chapter 1
From Adorno to Marx:
De-Aestheticizing the Modern

I. Realism, Modernism, and the Ideological Horizon

In an afterword to an anthology of critical exchanges between Brecht, Lukács, Bloch, Benjamin, and Adorno, Fredric Jameson argues that the continued relevance of these now-classical debates lies in an "aesthetic contradiction between 'Realism' and 'Modernism', whose navigation and renegotiation is still unavoidable for us today."[1] Despite the changes produced within late capitalism since the formation of what is now known as Critical Theory, both modernism and realism continue to represent opposed strategies of design for an aesthetic intended to articulate the inevitable temporal bifurcations of life itself—what Jameson refers to simply as "historicity." Whereas in the extinct epoch of "traditional society" aesthetics could restrict itself to the priestly vocation of administering a cult of beauty, on the assumption that the mechanisms of an eternal social order would not permit such a practice to be undermined, the ultimate decay of a totalizing Tradition, catalyzed by the onset of capitalism, has forced aesthetics to seek historical justification for itself. The revolutionary pace of life under capitalism means that everyone, artist and statesman alike, must operate as a *realist*, if only so as not to invite accusations of outdatedness. Modernism and realism are thus at the outset united in "lay[ing] claim to a binding relationship to the real itself" (*AP*, p. 198).

What, then, constitutes their difference? Jameson takes careful note of the fact that the simple and often uncritical generalization of certain privileged artistic genres—the novel, for Lukács; theatrical performance, for Brecht; the atonal

3

composition, for Adorno—may itself account for some of what only appears to be a properly aesthetic dispute. Discounting this kind of implicit generic advocacy (or perhaps seeing in it what is already the effect of an unspoken ideological commitment), it is nevertheless clear that profound contradiction persists and that it bears directly on the issue of *representation* as a specific mediation of the real. Bluntly stated, realism of the Lukácsian type operates on the presupposition that a recognized and universally shared practice of representation exists and that it "gives us the world" as it really is, so long as it serves what is from the outset an objectivist relation to the world *in practice*. Modernism—or, perhaps more accurately, a modernist realism—balks at this faith, stipulating, in the case of Brecht, the necessity for certain technical reforms of the representational medium. But more typically it adopts the radical rejectionist position of Adornian aesthetics, which completely reverses the Lukácsian position by equating the very universality and transparency of a positive schema of representation with the "totalitarian" opacity of the commodity fetish. Realism then, for Adornian modernism, can only be the achievement of a cognition that operates against representation—a cognition that, happily or unhappily, has no choice but to be "aesthetic."

With a deft stroke of historicizing synthesis that has become familiar to his readers, however, Jameson suggests that

> these apparently irreconcilable positions may prove to be two distinct and equally indispensable moments of the hermeneutic process itself—a first naive 'belief' in the density or presence of representation, and a later 'bracketing' of that experience in which the necessary distance of all language from what it claims to represent—its substitutions and displacements—are explored. (*AP*, p. 204)

What has seemed from both the modernist and realist standpoint to be a fundamental and inherently political opposition would, in this revised perspective, be better grasped as an aporia that "contains within its structure the crux of a history beyond which we have not yet passed" (*AP*, p. 213). In attempting to transcend or resolve the "debate," we thus only run up against what is, in so many words, the edge of that *ideological* horizon within which is given our very perception of opposition and any possible adherence to one or another counterposition.

II. Representation: The Ideology of the Horizon?

We can scarcely dispute the good sense of Jameson's simultaneously historical and critical foregrounding of the modernism/realism polemic nor deny that it is a real advance over past efforts to "resolve" it unilaterally. But in its impetus to historicize an intellectual configuration perhaps now given over to conceptual hypostasis, Jameson still effectively limits the targets of historicizing critique to certain theoretical *postures* and leaves hypostatically intact what must be the ground of their difference. This ground is that very discourse of aesthetics that centers around the concept of *representation*. Jameson's historicism permits us to explain how a certain critical position on representation is both generated by and *generative of* what appear to be counterpositions, but it does not explain, nor deem it necessary to explain, the specific appropriateness of an aesthetics of representation as such to the problem of historicity. Yet might not the very possibility of historicity-as-the-real to be given as an object endowed with presence for a distinctly aesthetic (that is, perceptualized) subjectivity—might not this possibility be itself the product of a historic conjuncture, however broadly epochal? Does not the *practice* of representation, in contrast to the naturalizing generality of its concept, always articulate a subject-object dialectic that is itself historically grounded and mediated? And might it not turn out that it is by means of the very operation of posing historicity as a problem for an aesthetics of representation that representation is rendered exempt from historicizing critique?

If it is true that Jameson's line of reasoning commits us to the uncritical retention of a naturalized theory of representation, it must also and without hesitation be admitted that the same ideological reflex operates in *any* theoretical discourse that identifies itself as aesthetic or that treats representation and language as interchangeable concepts. No matter how powerfully and radically historical the system of explanation we employ in order to wrest a specific instance of representation (a novel, a painting) from the inverted and hypostatic place of its self-identity, the effect is still to leave intact and in position the metaphysical *moment* of representation as such, outside and prior to its historical realization in a concrete subject-object dialectic. Into this moment history cannot penetrate without violating the rules of the aesthetic discourse with which it has agreed to coexist. The idea that the very mechanisms of representation might themselves undergo modification in time and space seems laughable and counterintuitive. In the continuous movement of history and discourse, something, after all, has to remain fixed.

But by proceeding too swiftly with the Jamesonian historicization of the realism/modernism problematic as ideological aporia, we run the risk of obscuring, in the name of a conjunctural reading, the real and radical depth of the aporetic fix. Something very much like the idea of a dialectized progression from a "naive" to a "critical" practice of representation, to which Jameson assigns a hermeneutic meaning, is already implicitly worked out in the aesthetic theory of Adorno—and perhaps that is why Jameson's final projection of a "new realism" that would "resist the power of reification in consumer society" in essence repeats an Adornian argument (*AP*, p. 212). In Adorno, as, to a lesser extent, in the aesthetics of the proponents of Critical Theory who follow his lead (Horkheimer, Marcuse, Lowenthal), we find clearly articulated the theoretical consciousness of a *crisis in representation* that must seek the reason for its existence outside its own formal dimensions in a dialectic of history. Adorno's defense of modernism thus differs radically not only from its obvious Lukácsian antinomy but from the naive modernisms (Russian formalist, Poundian, and "garden variety" surrealist) that stigmatize representational realism as little more than a worn-out optical tool that must be traded in for a new one. It is, rather, the attempt to supplant such naturalizing ideologies of representation with a dialectized and historical critique which we see consistently exerting itself in tracts like *The Dialectic of Enlightenment* and Adorno's aesthetic criticism proper.

The thesis of a *historical* crisis in representation perhaps emerges most powerfully and unreservedly in the opening lines of the well-known fragment of *Minima Moralia*, fragment 94, entitled "All the World's Not a Stage": "The coming extinction of art is prefigured in the increasing impossibility of representing historical events."[2] Adorno's immediate target is Brecht's *Arturo Ui* and its implicit claim to effect both a critical and realistic representation of Hitlerian fascism. Adorno adamantly denies this claim but not, as a naive modernism might prompt us to suppose, on the basis of a bad aesthetics. The "impossibility" to which Brecht inevitably falls victim is in the essence of the object itself—fascism—as a historical entity. Fascism, the "coming-to-itself of society as such," cannot become the object of a realistic portrayal that follows the standard aesthetic strategy of representing "historical events," a strategy that Adorno summarizes by referring to its two alternative principles of "psychology" and "infantilism" (the former is typified in the nineteenth-century "political" dramas of Schiller; the latter refers to Brecht's own representational tactic of "schematic parables"). No amount of technical innovation or "estrangement" can overcome this inexorable falsification in which is expressed the decisive failure of an aesthetics of representation to master the "essential abstractness of what really happens." "The impossibility of portraying Fascism springs from the fact that in it, as in its contemplation, subjective freedom no longer exists."[3]

III. Adorno and Critical Metaphysics

Reading fragment 94 strictly on its own terms, we might derive from it something like the following line of critique: fascism, insofar as it has come to typify the synthetic social formation of advanced monopoly capitalism (what Critical Theory refers to variously as the "culture industry," the "administered universe," and "totalitarianism"), forces upon the aesthetic practice of representation the realization that, despite the assurances of its self-consciousness as theory, it is a practice without a real, historically existing subject. In other words, history has undermined the subjective immediacy of the social individual who might once have made it possible for the aesthetic strategies of psychology and infantilism to realistically portray "what really happens." In place of this socially and historically falsified subject there stands another, of radically different dimensions, in whom a different theory and practice of aesthetic realism is implied and upon whom alone can such an aesthetic be erected.

Such is not, however, the line ultimately taken by Adorno, either in *Minima Moralia*, where the "dissolution of the subject in collective society" is given an accent of unmitigated and absolute degradation, or in those instances in which the more familiar and affirmative principles of Adornian aesthetics are expounded. The one ray of dialectical hope that is allowed to penetrate the neo-Hegelian pessimism of fragment 94—the truth that "total unfreedom can be recognized, but not represented"—holds out the promise of rehabilitation not to society but to art. It is the "autonomous" artwork as such, epitomized in the modernist tradition of a Schoenberg, a Beckett, a Kafka, and so on, that makes good the metaphysical investment in representation by refusing any subjective or social mediation whatsoever.

Most of us are familiar with the general outlines of Adornian aesthetics as the defense of modernist and vanguard art in the name of a universal and abstract *negation*. For contemporary exponents of the modernism-as-"lament over reification"[4] doctrine we need look no further than to Jameson himself.[5] Less obvious, however—and it is this line of critique I shall attempt to pursue here—is how, in the course of constructing this "dialectical" rationale for modernism over and against the naive "mechanics" of Lukácsian mimesis, the in itself valid critical premise of a historical crisis in representation becomes the point of departure for its own ideological inversion in a reconstituted metaphysics of representation. Does not the historically falsified subject of representation as it resides uncritically and hypostatically in naive realism simply become the doubly falsified "autonomy" preached by a Critical Theory that alludes to historical reality only in order to abdicate its materialist injunctions? In place of the representational metaphysics of realism, what do we obtain but the same metaphysics shorn of its "psychology" and bearing the descriptive title of "negation"? Representation, subject to historical interrogation, seems merely to reemerge conceptually intact as its "dialectical" Other. Is this not perhaps an ideological reflex action of modernism itself? Adorno no doubt takes this ideology to the point of its critical self-consciousness by positing representation as a historically fallen consciousness, but in the end he reaestheticizes critique and is thus reclaimed by the ideology being criticized.

IV. "The Revolution That Never Happened"

What should be the approach of a Marxist aesthetics toward this discursive and ideological fixation? In another, but fundamentally analogous, context—that of criticizing the Althusserian effort to detach literature from ideology by making the former out to be the figural and critical self-consciousness of the latter—Tony Bennett has stated flatly that "a historical and materialist theory of the production of different forms of writing demands a prior break with the concerns of bourgeois aesthetics."[6] For Bennett this is to be accomplished by breaking with formally and politically "essentialist" ideologies of the *text*. Transposing "text" to the broader philosophical category of "representation," we may find ourselves in provisional agreement with Bennett but at the same time constrained to admit that the means of effecting such a break are not immediately available to criticism. Bennett, who rightfully exposes the idealism of ascribing a critical or even revolutionary agency to literature as such (the same idealism of Adornian aesthetics on the "negative" properties of "autonomous" art), does not evade the problem by reascribing this agency to *criticism*.[7] This points us in the right direction but does not rid us of the modernist ideological baggage of "bourgeois aesthetics." For it cannot be automatically supposed that critics possess the direct theoretical means of producing the desired "break" without recuperating those very metaphysical inversions that deposit themselves as part of the theoretical discourse of representation. Missing is a materialist theoretical tradition in which to carry out the critique of aesthetic representation in accordance with an intuitive historical consciousness of representational crisis. We face something like the situation described by Lukács, in the self-critical preface to his *Theory of the Novel*, as the "fusion of a 'left' ethics with a 'right' epistemology."[8]

But as critics we may, nevertheless, have access to certain tactical alternatives. One such tactic is obliquely suggested by a remark of Alfred Sohn-Rethel's in the introduction to his major work, *Intellectual and Manual Labour*. Sohn-Rethel, a generational cohort of Bloch, Horkheimer, Kracauer, Benjamin, and Adorno—whose critical focus on epistemology did not, significantly, lead him to share their aesthetic concerns—affirms the work of these theoreticians, along with that of Marcuse and of Lukács, as a "new development of Marxist thought."[9] But in a telling contrast to Jameson's aesthetically recuperative assessment of this generation, Sohn-Rethel writes that this development

> evolved as the theoretical and ideological superstructure of the revolution that never happened. In it re-echo the thunder of the gun battle for the Marstall in Berlin at Christmas 1918, and the shooting of the Spartacus rising in the following winter. The paradoxical condition of this ideological movement may help to explain its almost exclusive preoccupation with superstructural questions, and the conspicuous lack of concern for the material and economic base that should have been underlying it.[10]

What emerges here is the notion of a theoretical discourse of modern aesthetics as, in effect, a displaced politics. The crisis in representation that evinces the various and conflicting efforts to produce a historicized aesthetics—an aesthetics of the *real*—would itself, according to such an analysis, be read as the effect of a political crisis so radical as to resist its direct theoretical and critical appropriation. History must be made to compensate, on the level of the superstructure, that which it withholds from life in its politico-economic dimension.

Against this "superstructuralism," Sohn-Rethel trains Critical Theory back onto the analysis of the commodity and the opening sections of *Capital*. In *Intellectual and Manual Labour* we can trace the "revolution that never happened" in a possible transcendence of an exchange-based social nexus, which, given the political circumstances, fails to complete itself—a state of "dual social synthesis."

But Marx, too, had occasion to reflect on revolutionary derailments and their consequences for representational truths of history and politics. I refer to the defeat of the social revolutionary aspirations of the Parisian proletariat in 1848 and the subsequent triumph of a populist counterrevolution in the coup d'état of 1851. The relevant text—to which I now turn—is, of course, *The Eighteenth Brumaire of Louis Bonaparte*, a text that, like the *Minima Moralia* fragment, speaks of a history "painted grey on grey," a "history without events."[11]

V. Adorno and the Eighteenth Brumaire

What makes the text of the *Eighteenth Brumaire* tactically advantageous vis-à-vis modernism and the apparent political impasse thrown up by its Adornian theorization is the peculiar way in which it suggests its own aesthetic reading even as it refuses to become the inscription of a discourse of aesthetics per se. The *Eighteenth Brumaire* points to the existence of what might be modernism's authentic subtext, without itself taking a decisively modernist leap into antirepresentationalism. Thus Adorno might very well find a way of affirming men's "making their own history . . . not just as they please," for what men themselves make, as a result of their precontainment in the given representations of the object of their activity, turns out indeed to be History as that same supremely alienated "course of the world," that "coming to itself of society as such" that is already inscribed in the "given circumstances"—the "unmittelbar, vorgefundenen, gegebenen und uberlieferten Umständen."[12] Conversely, the inevitability of counterrevolution and thus the motive for a taking of refuge in aesthetics—for Adorno, the total assimilation of the subject by the "administered universe"—may convey the more typically Hegelian sense of a negation of the negation, making counterrevolution the very enabling condition of revolution itself. This is the conclusion drawn by Marx in the opening paragraph of *Class Struggles in France*, according to which it is not the revolution per se that is defeated in 1848–49 but rather its "pre-revolutionary appendages."[13] Marx's affirmation of a residual agency, a revolutionary subject empowered to redeem and transform itself in the face of its initial failure to penetrate a representational feign, becomes for Adornian modernism an outdated article of faith. But in the tradition of the *Eighteenth Brumaire* even this skepticism may be considered as simply

another "clearing away," a negation of naive expectation that must itself be negated in order for a more effective strategy to assume its place.

It has, of course, become conventional to distinguish the class struggles of the
nineteenth century, even after the defeats of 1848, from a more properly "modern" social antagonism in which the moment of conflict has receded from the
locus classicus of the barricade and positioned itself within the realm of an ideology that, according to its Althusserian mapping, marks its hegemonic success
or failure in the constitution of social subjects as such. "Late capitalism," as
reckoned by certain theoretical currents, has rendered the old strategies, including the Leninist, obsolete—or, at best, contingent upon a rupturing of the max-
imally reifying totality of "consumer society." The *Eighteenth Brumaire* would
thus come to be read as a theoretical reflection of nineteenth-century struggles
that anticipates the ultimate tendency toward hypostasis and reification of given
categorizations of the political but that mistakenly ascribes defeat and counterrevolution to the immaturity of the proletariat—its need for a political theory, or
system of representation, that more truly reflects the content of its own political
interests as "social revolution"—rather than to its ideological entrapment in an
increasingly abstract economic mechanism that brackets political agency itself.
To be sure, Marx's "mistake" is, to a greater or lesser degree, interlaced with
good historical reckoning, depending on where and when this advanced mechanism is thought to commence functioning. We can even concur with Lenin's tracing (in *State and Revolution*) of the practical triumph of the Paris Commune to
the theoretical lessons drawn from 1848 by Marx and the vanguard sectors of the
working-class movement, and perhaps allow 1917 its place in this special dialectic of enlightenment, and yet still explain what appears to be the crippling limi-
tation of this theoretical odyssey as being due to, in Adorno's phrase, "the essential abstractness of what really happens." "Barbaric meaninglessness"
overwhelms everything in the end—as it must if, as the modernist unconscious
seems to demand, some means of allowing theory to contain practice is required
for society to "make its own history." The bracketing game would, then, be won
at last by Adorno, whose fragment 94 becomes the postscriptural rewriting of the
Eighteenth Brumaire in an age of mass-produced and electronic Bonapartism.
The triumph of fascism, in its cultural if not always in its political content, pro-
nounces the final verdict on all political attempts to break the logic of a reified
social existence, the political now being understood to comprise any and every
theoretical and practical impulse that must employ the representational categories
of that which it desires to transform or overthrow. "What appears to be the triumph of subjective rationality, the subjection of all reality to logical formalism,
is paid for by the obedient subjection of reason to what is *directly given*."[14] The
opportunity for escape offers itself only in those spaces in which reason and representation cease to perform a specific function but still postulate the real in its
negativity. It is only here that the reified world can be both comprehended and, as

it were, mastered by the subject. This is the complex agency identified by Adorno as modern art: it is the modern aesthetic alone that is finally empowered to refuse total containment in the *given*, which, as in Adorno's and Horkheimer's phrase, extends the vitiating necessity for the present to represent itself in terms of the past to a virtual embargo on a theoretical praxis that posits anything beyond its own sheer negativity.

Within the enclosed space of late capitalism's "totalitarian" ideology, then, a modernist aesthetics filters out as the vestige of an autonomy whose nineteenth-century version was a concrete historical subject: a revolutionary proletariat. The place of this subject in Marx's discourse shows up in Adorno as the formal possibility of a modern art. That is why art, for Adorno, cannot simply be placed at the service of the proletariat; rather, art must redeem the historical failure of the proletariat by opening up a tiny negative and emancipatory fissure in a history without revolutionary agencies.

It is within the ambit of a certain "vulgar" modernism (inhabiting the discursive space set aside by dominant institutions for the proprietorship of "aesthetics") that this narrative architecture best conceals itself. The relative security of its hiding place is approximately verified in the uncontested ease with which the discourse of "the Arts" lays claim to the language of the avant-garde. In "modern times" it is the artists and poets who write the manifestos and rebel against the tyranny of the given. Without ceasing to merge with this discursive norm at its root, Adornian Critical Theory in effect serves as its radical social conscience. Adorno's is a *critical* modernism; and if it dubs over the *Eighteenth Brumaire* with an aestheticized defeatism, it does so with seemingly good theoretical reasoning and on the best of social-philosophical authorities—the labor theory of value and the critique of commodity fetishism as expounded in the first volume of *Capital*. In an intepretive maneuver that has come to typify the basic line of cultural theory associated with the Frankfurt school, Adorno identifies the essentially Kantian aesthetic principle of the noninstrumental with the Marxian category of the authentic and concrete as (use) value unmediated by exchange. An aesthetics of the noninstrumental undergoes a social radicalization in becoming an aesthetics of the "nonfungible." Modern art thus retains at least an anticapitalist aspect (if not a revolutionary one) in its conscious "resistance" to the reification (instrumentalization) wrought by exchange. And where revolution has failed for the foreseeable future, modern art can measure what are at least real, if small, victories in the capacity of its works to "hibernate" through the long winter of counterrevolutionary ascendancy. *Capital* is read as much for its political abstraction as for its concrete analysis of capital itself. Its theoretical terms, transposed into a discourse of aesthetics, become the renarrativized players of a nineteenth-century drama whose protagonist and political setting have been purged but whose plot continues to be played out. Even in *Minima Moralia*, where art itself is about to become "extinct," the apparent hopelessness of the situation is measured in the absence, if not of a traditional revolutionary hero, then of a ''writer'' whose ''most urgent task'' it is to overcome the ''insolubilities'' of representation. As the readers implicit in this familiar narrative, which bears the weight of a prophesied doom and makes it tolerable, we all know that this ''writer'' will succeed and that he will do so by becoming ''autonomous art.'' Aesthetics reinvents what a traditional political narrative is no longer able to convey: the ideological presence of the empowered subject.

VI. Nineteenth Century/Twentieth Century: One-Dimensional Historicism

If the tactic of reading Adornian aesthetic theory as a twentienth-century, late capitalist rewriting of the *Eighteenth Brumaire*—as a displaced vector of criticism elicited by a counterrevolutionary inversion—works at all, it is in its allowance for a residual narrative of agency in both Adornian and modernist theory in general. The transfer of agency from a ''conventional'' historical subject to a ''modern'' equivalent in the negative instrumentality of ''autonomous'' art may thus at least be thought of as carrying out the terms of a discursive protocol. The twentieth century must, after all, bid adieu to the nineteenth in terms the latter can understand.

But suppose that we are not ready for this leave-taking. Suppose, if only for the sake of argument, that it is precisely this suspiciously innocent scenario of sorrowful farewell, so expertly played by the author of *Minima Moralia*, that serves as modernism's subtlest ideological blind. Our conventional, historicist sense of ''the nineteenth century'' is, to be sure, one of irrevocable loss: ''They will come no more, / the old men with beautiful manners.''[15] What can be more *past* than a nineteenth century that is the equivalent, in the conventional historicist imagination, of one's own childhood? May we not suspect the hand of modernist aesthetics itself in what otherwise seems merely a natural and premodernist chronological retrospect?

With these suspicions in mind, we might expect to advance more successfully toward an ideology critique of modernism by reading the *Eighteenth Brumaire* within a field in which the conventional historicist polarities are inverted. This would mean observing the ways in which Marx's text fails to exhaust itself within the system of relative weights and measures, proposed, mutatis mutandis, by Adorno's antireifying aestheticism. We have already seen how, by permitting the Marxian discourse of 1848 to be bracketed by its supposedly modern equivalent in the critique of reified culture, a process of substitution and cancellation is initiated whose end result is the precipitation of a transcendent agency, that of the aesthetic proper. But here we must remind ourselves that it is merely the locus for a nonpolitical, postrepresentational subject that results from the Adornian rewriting of the *Eighteenth Brumaire*; the identification of this ideal occupant with the aesthetic per se cannot claim any necessary determination from within the terms of the rewriting.

How, then, do we proceed to *invert*, in effect, the modernist rewriting of the *Eighteenth Brumaire*? The obvious inclination simply to rewrite the history of late capitalism within the discursive or narrative paradigms of a nineteenth-century *grand récit* of class struggle, thus restoring the locus of agency to the political, may have the advantage of drawing fire from outright idealist and defeatist quarters, but, as already stated, it can also only have the effect of impoverishing critique, of positing a "nineteenth-century" present tense in which the realities of twentieth-century monopoly and state capitalist ideology are themselves always already hypostatically present.

To reduce the Adornian critical project to just another "prerevolutionary appendage" thrown up by a tardy dialectic can only, at this juncture, beg the question of Adorno as ideology, in effect hypostasizing it as well. For in positing a "nineteenth century" cleansed of "decadent" modernism, modernity itself becomes reinscribed as a repressed but unavoidable Other (this is the familiar ruse that offends deconstruction). A "classic" nineteenth century, whether aesthetic or political, would, after all, tend toward closure only in the discourse of a modernism that abjures it—or reads it as "farce."

It is, I would suggest, already the ideological imprint of hegemonized modernism that "nineteenth-" and "twentieth-century" "tragedy" and "farce," "classic" and "modern" appear to us as structurally dependent antinomies, their relation that of "specularity." And so it is within the historicist *récit* framing *Minima Moralia* as well: one mourns the loss of a humane "yet then," which must, however, always register as a loss a priori if the affirmative meaning of a modernity to which one is already committed is to be affirmed.

An inversion of the modernized *Eighteenth Brumaire* would then have to begin in the attempt to *subvert* the specular logic that simply reinscribes the modernized historicist imagination while reversing its ethical polarity. Indeed, it might now be argued that the Adornian rewriting of Marx whose outlines I have sketched derives its characteristic social pessimism not only from the actual political defeats implicit in fascism and the culture industry but likewise, and just as importantly, from the seeming *theoretical* aporias of the specular. Thus, in the introduction to the *Dialectic of Enlightenment*:

> When examining its own guilty conscience, thought has to forgo not only the affirmative use of scientific and everyday conceptual language, but just as much that of the opposition. There is no longer available any form of linguistic expression which has not tended towards accommodation to dominant currents of thoughts.[16]

A "language . . . of the opposition" that "tends towards accommodation," and so forth—the residual terms of a nineteenth-century political narrative surface, in quite typical fashion, amid the critique of a state of affairs no longer subject to political agencies. "Opposition" is merely the fictional name for a negation that cannot find a foothold outside the logic of positivity in which it is generated. All that exists is the "one-dimensionality" of a reflecting surface—all, that is, except the "aesthetic dimension."

But are the "given circumstances" of the *Eighteenth Brumaire* also this one-dimensional reflecting surface? To read/rewrite them as such, modernism must propose a medium that can channel the "archaic" nineteenth-century language of politics and revolution (the only slightly displaced accusations and calls to action, the proclamation of a present "ripe" for revolutionary synthesis, etc.) into that which is really "modern" in Marx's text, namely, its theoretical moment. The modern sense of the *Eighteenth Brumaire*, as generally of a Marxian "text of History," must start with the premise that there are, to begin with, *two* texts: one that merely reflects in its morality and its literary devices an outmoded set of social relations and ideological limits, and a second that leaps out of its romantic integument and suspends the claims of an outmoded practice in the pursuit of theoretical abstraction. The latter text is, of course, not the *Eighteenth Brumaire* but *Capital*, not manifesto but critique. The *Eighteenth Brumaire* could accordingly convey a fully modern signification by producing this theoretical abstraction independently of its narrative apparatus, thus causing its narrative or ideological text to detach itself from its referent and acquire an allegorical value. This abstraction would be "Bonapartism," the nineteenth century's predesignation of reification and the culture industry. The days of February and June 1848, the election of Louis Bonaparte, the coup d'état of 2 December 1851—in all such events there would be registered only the loss of an autonomy that has, *ab origine*, figured as an abstract telos present in these events as their final historical outcome. "Men make their own history" under "given circumstances" in which, however, there is always already inscribed the logic that will alienate the results of their activity.

VII. Praxis as a "Farce"

Subverting the specular thus becomes a question of how Marx's text might be made to resist not its own readability as an instance of theory but the process whereby its very theoretical reading engulfs and, in effect, suspends its direct relation to a praxis of historical subjects. Let us start with what is perhaps the text's principal *vulnerability* to specularism—this is the ultrafamiliar allegory of history repeating itself, "the first time as tragedy, the second time as farce." As a discursive strategy in the service of theory, the language of tragedy and farce can immediately be seen to suggest the suspension of praxis by positing a *spec-*

tator who views the historical action taking place on stage without taking an active part. In the course of theatrical representation, the spectator must suspend his own activity—otherwise he is in danger of ceasing to remain a spectator, and representation as such breaks down. Moreover, as the spectator of a *farce*, he must be able not only to identify the purely mimetic character of what happens on stage, in opposition to his own self-identical spectatorship, but also to confirm the discrepancy between what the players subjectively intend and the objective outcome of their activity as measured against a standard of preexisting meaning. Those who act out a farce do not grasp the true meaning of what they do—but what makes a farce a farce is not this alone but the fact that this authenticity of meaning is already a property accessible to the non-actor who witnesses the spectacle. In relation to this spectator's meaning, "farce" attains the status of representation in approximately its modernist sense: a meaninglessness that adopts meaningful form and in which the mediating relation of subject and object is reversed, linking the "actions" of the dramatis personae to an agency outside themselves.

Such representation takes a literally textual form in the *Eighteenth Brumaire*: the constitutional articles, legislative acts, ministerial decisions and executive decrees that add up to "that work of art, the bourgeois republic" (*EB*, p. 121). The "periods" which mark the subdivisions of Marx's narrative (see Marx's list at the end of section 6) in essence indicate the displacement of each successive attempt to exercise authority by signifying it (the "force of words") toward an abstract power that violates the very terms of the signifying contract, using authority's representational conventions unfailingly to its advantage. Each of the successively farcical protagonists—Pure Republicans, Democratic Republicans, the Party of Order, and Bonaparte himself—produces its own grotesque demise by substituting real conflict with its quixotic representation, as defined not by the actual relations of force but by the *letter* of the law. Pursuit of a purely textual legitimacy generates a situation in which the illegitimate asserts itself without any formal or legal restrictions. After all, on the level of pure representation, what inherent superiority can a law of universal suffrage have over a wall-placard pronunciamento announcing a state of siege?

Authority as the mere representationality of power is powerless, and what renders it so is the capacity of power itself to establish and reproduce itself, so to speak, in abstraction from the level on which it is signified. Abstract power, or the "independent" Bonapartist state machine, takes on the properties of a subject for which constitutions, decrees, and so forth, are no longer binding but, rather, the manipulable and in themselves meaningless forms of a metalanguage that this subject "speaks" at will. The legal subjects specified in the letter of the law—subjects whom the players in the bourgeois farce believe themselves to be—become the mere animated fictions of a staged drama.

At this point the allegory of farce is naturally amplified in a manner that equates the grotesque play of representation with the structure of History itself as a given *past*, while the spectator's unmediated access to meaning in the revelation of an abstract state power becomes, as part of the same equation, access to an absolute and disjunctive, nonrepetitive *present*. Representation acquires the seemingly inexorable quality of being "archaic" — not only past but arbitrary and extrinsic with respect to the present. The poetry of revolution, or of History as the present, "can only be drawn from the future," but, as Adorno teaches us, the "essential abstractness of what really happens" already "rebuts the aesthetic image," rendering the very representational form of this poetry obsolete. The future can be drawn only as an accelerating process of totalizing abstraction and alienation, "incommensurable" with what society already knows of itself from the History that has engendered it. Gaining access to this present from which conventional historical time has been purged requires the spectatorial detachment of a critical-theoretical subjectivity. Such, at least, would be the ultimate judgment of the "modern" *Eighteenth Brumaire*, a text prefiguring the Adornian aesthetics of late capitalism in its capacity to foreground the narrative and representational codes of History by simply reading them as one would the text of a farce — but a text that does not thereby cease to write itself as History.

VIII. "Farce" as praxis

Earlier I spoke of modernism's need for a medium in which to channel the narrative body of the *Eighteenth Brumaire*, and in general any narrative by means of which a historical agency is represented, into a rewriting that can affirm the theoretical unity of Marx's text. The allegory of farce would appear to supply this medium and has the obvious advantage of deriving from the text itself. Moreover, farce suggests Marx's own perception of the need to foreground representation in a manner that is detached and "theoretical," whereas tragedy entails a cathartic encumbrance of theory. We might even appeal to farce, or the ironical stance it presupposes, as to a sort of primitive act of "negation." Like a modern artist, Marx makes possible the cognition of his object — History — by turning its representations against themselves.

But the allegorical possibilities of farce cannot be so easily managed. The seemingly unlimited vulnerability of representation to a displacement that renders meaningless its particular and local theory of meaning also threatens to displace the spectatorial subject who derives the farce effect. For the simple positing of the locus of semiotic authority outside any given system of correspondences does not *ipso facto* secure the spectatorial subject in this position. Without becoming part of the drama he "sees," the spectator is nevertheless not immune to the bifurcation that places him before himself as the notorious "fourth wall" of the theater — not immune to that agency that represents *him* in the service of some more fundamentally incommensurable and alien power whose abstraction exceeds his own rather limited theoretical detachment. The spectator must, after all, become that particular spectator that the spectacle demands, just as the "educated" audience of a Hollywood film or a television soap opera must allow marginal credit to these representational schemes before it can conclude that such stuff is mere hype. The spectatorial subject, whose claim to exist outside the logic repetition requires an identification of the nonrepetitive (the modern) with the cognitive moment of appropriating the "hidden meaning," cannot thereby be said to have foregrounded the narrative that makes this particular spectatorial agency appear as naturally and spontaneously given. The highly seductive image of a spectatorial vantage, equated with the place of theory in cognition and cutting across the specular dimension of a false autonomy (a degraded and false mode of agency) can do no more than multiply the levels of representation.

There is, of course, an inevitable sense in which the structural place of the narrator in any narrative discourse lends itself to this imagery, since the *past* of recounted events presupposes a minimally contiguous *present* from which to recount them. It would be pointless to try to "save" Marx from falling into this place in the *Eighteenth Brumaire*. But what is the critical status of this "present" in Marx's text?

In Adorno's fragment 94, which deems impossible a *narrative* present in which "what really happens" can take on a recognizable form, the present itself is affirmatively implied as that which, out of its own essence, eludes representation and assumes cognitive shape only for critical-theoretical consciousness. "Events" give no hint as to the authentic meaning of the present for a social subject. "Events" can inform can by way of a negation that posits their radical incommensurability—an incommensurability that resists circumvention by such representational schemes as those deployed by the realism of a Brecht or a Schiller. A concrete and conscious existence in the present, in an activated mode of history, is a subjective privilege possible only for those modern, "autonomous" works of art that grasp the "essential abstractness" of the real through an absolute negation unmediated by concepts, the latter immediacy being the condition of their own protection against a totalizing abstraction. (Somehow, of course, it must also be the privilege of the Critical Theorist enabled to affirm this fact.) Hidden in the unfathomable concreteness of modern art is thus not only the unique formula for autonomous conduct in the face of the totalitarianism of representationally mediated knowledge—the only way of really uniting theory with an authentic instance of praxis—but also the lived experience of freedom as such.

Adorno's investment of the aethetic with what amounts to a capacity and responsibility to make good the humanist value of subjective freedom represents, in ways already discussed, a concomitant divestment of a political and "revolutionary" accountability for this same value. Politics must inevitably disappoint humanism because its very nature as a discourse of historical agency, as a narrative of "events" in which agents of a specific historical type effectively play out the parts of theory and praxis in a dramatic unity that is dubbed revolution, forces it into contradiction with the conclusions of social theory at the level of the economy and of culture. Such conclusions, in the estimation of Critical Theory, restrict the exercise of autonomy to the abstract and inhuman subjectivity of monopoly capitalist society itself, as manifest in its culture industry. Even the *Eighteenth Brumaire* can be made to appear as a precursive authority for this disavowal, which is later reflected in the focus on categories that apparently exclude a political agency in the discourse of *Capital*. The sublation of the political within the aesthetic permits accommodation of these conclusions but without thereby canceling entirely the theoretical possibility of resisting and opposing the "purely inhuman" within the disjunctive present that it imposes. Aesthetics recuperates a present, a History in the revolutionary sense, in which freedom can, theoretically at least, be given as something subjective and immediate.

Having said this, however, I must immediately counter that Marx, simply by virtue of observing the displacement of representation in the political sphere from "what really happens" does not thereby reproduce this same *aesthetic* desire to escape from the mediacy of repetition. If, in the *Eighteenth Brumaire*, the present remains concealed in the past, conceivable only as a representation of the given, there is no indication of a subsequent commitment to the restoration of History in something corresponding to its "original state." The construction of Marx's sarcastic, theatrical critique of the bourgeois counterrevolution suggests, rather, the *absence of a present*, which, far from being a merely cognitive problem, implicates a state of *practical* perplexity. The text is, indeed, quite clear on this:

> During the years 1848–51 French society has made up for the studies and experiences—albeit by a method which is condensed because it is revolutionary—which, in a regular, so to speak, textbook course of development should have preceded the February Revolution if it was to be more than a ruffling of the surface. Society now seems to have fallen back behind its point of departure; it has in truth first to create for itself the revolutionary point of departure, the situation, the relations, the conditions under which alone modern revolution becomes serious. (*EB*, pp. 13–14)

Here it will not do to simply accuse Marx of investing "society" with the attributes of a romanticized political agency, of falling for the farce that he exposes elsewhere, because the very concept of society here articulated already problematizes the identity of class subject and historical agency. Society is not automatically assumed to reside in the representations that appeal to its concept. In the extraordinary contrast between "bourgeois revolutions, like those of the eighteenth century" with "proletarian revolutions, like those of the nineteenth" (which follows on the above passage), the difference consists in how differing instances of societal motion, generated out of existing states of social synthesis, not only structure the specific agencies that make revolution—and counter-revolution—but actually produce the specific form of temporal mediation in which activity is constituted. The sheer descriptive and stylistic force of this paragraph may indeed tend to obscure the complex order of difference that it constructs. That which lends a consecutively carnivalized and depressed character to "bourgeois revolution" is the fundamental consubstantiality of the latter with the present as an achieved state, the obligatory bond of the bourgeois revolution to the presentness of what has already happened. Spectacular events typify this revolution, not through any quality of tragic impetuosity inherent in its protagonists (on the contrary!) but because the event-form itself subsists on the representation of activity as necessarily complete and self-identical. "On the other hand, proletarian revolutions . . . criticize themselves constantly, interrupt themselves continually in their own course, come back to the apparently accomplished in order to begin it afresh" (EB, p. 14). Proletarian revolutions, that is, proceed within a mode of *repetition* that, in contrast to the counterrevolutionary entailments of bourgeois repetitiveness, creates the conditions for a revolutionary present that reaches a state of completion only through its very *uneventfulness* and in which completion is already the mark of its passage into something else. Activity is never securely itself and cannot be truthfully represented in the accomplished act of its antiheroic class agent. The repetition of "proletarian revolution" progressively whittles its way toward a present that, paradoxically, can never be the quantitative function of these unevents, since past and present have already ceased to exist along a mediated continuum. It is by means of this complex and contradictory articulation of agencies and counteragencies, of representation in a permanent state of uncertain reference, that a "situation [is] created which makes all turning back impossible." (EB, p. 14). The moment in which the plane of representation is held up and confronted with its actually false and arbitrary nature, in which the scandal of representation calls attention to itself, is literally something for which there is no time.

To in any way identify the representational structure of farce with a state of historical and political autonomy would be to violate the very precondition of Adornian aesthetic critique. In Adorno, autonomy is presupposed as the exclusive privilege of a nonrepetitive "recognition"—that is, of a spectatorship. That this identity is, on the contrary, clearly operant throughout the *Eighteenth Brumaire* can be explained as the effect of Marx's narration of "events" without reference to a self-identical, established, and spectatorial present against which their "meaninglessness" can be conclusively affirmed. Revolutionary social activity, praxis, the "making" of History—these do not lose meaning as a result of being the merely derivative repetitions of the past-as-given because *they never take place anywhere but within the space of this "given" itself.* History as farce lacks a spectator, since it at no point supplies the temporal platform from which a spectatorial subject can cease to represent and commence to watch. Farce must itself "create . . . the conditions under which [it can] becom[e] serious." To conclude, on the strength of this, that history therefore lacks any subject would be to refuse the subject only that autonomy that presents itself in the dominant, spectatorial imagery of "theory."

IX. Proleptic Tradition

Now—if the mode of repetition designated as farce in the *Eighteenth Brumaire* in fact refuses to define the space of the absent historical subject demanded by modernism, then this must also affect the ability of modernism to base itself in the text by reading in it a "theoretical" refusal of its own narrative—or, perhaps more aptly, journalistic—level. We recall that according to this more general modernist sense of the text, the *Eighteenth Brumaire* must initially be split into two disjunctive modes: one that ties it to the immediacy of the nineteenth-century present that it analyzes, thus conferring upon it the narrative form of events themselves; and another that attempts to distance itself from this narrative encumbrance so as to construct its deeper social and historical sources theoretically. These sources are what later come to be identified in the familiar analytical categories of a Marxist theory of politics outlined in Lenin's *State and Revolution*: the state as a historically given form of class dictatorship and revolution as the "smashing" of this state to make way for the ascendancy of a new class. According to the modernist *Eighteenth Brumaire*, however, these categories are themselves only the more refined conceptualizations of the events that they interpret and project; they are master narratives, which ultimately commit theory only to a higher level of the representation/repetition syndrome that it desires to avoid in the more immediate conjuncture. If it wants to overcome this retrograde specularity, modernism must then interpret the categories of a Marxist politics as the inevitably premodern, nineteenth-century form selected by the more fully critical and modern concepts of commodity reification and its antithesis in an aesthetics of "recognition." The *Eighteenth Brumaire* is thus read as a prefigurative text about reification and aesthetic negation that simply lacks the adequate categories in which to formulate this authentic theoretical content. The "events" that it analyzes are equivalent to forms of representation that already exemplify in a farcical "comedy of state" what is later to afflict society as a monolithic culture industry.

We are, again, persuaded by this view so long as we do not question its preliminary judgment that the Marxian narrative observes the limitations and conventions of a familiar form of journalism. But like the bourgeois revolution of which it is an offspring, journalistic representation must itself derive from a constitution of the present as an already achieved state. One reads journalistic prose not only to find out "what really happens" but more fundamentally to confirm that what happens does not in any way alter what already is. But, to repeat my specific interpretive claim, Marx in the *Eighteenth Brumaire* is never, strictly speaking, engaged in the narration of past events, however immediately past, but rather in the analysis of events that inherently fail to add up to a present. The *Eighteenth Brumaire* does not "narrate" in the sense modernism would impute to it; rather, it recounts and arranges—periodizes—the "events" of 1848–51 in an order that brings into relief the contradictory relation they bear toward what are their own spontaneous auto-narrations:

> During the June days all classes and parties had united in the *party of Order* against the proletarian class as the *party of Anarchy*, of Socialism, of Communism. They had "saved" society from the "enemies of society." They had given out the watchwords of the old society, *"property, family, religion, order,"* to their army as passwords and had proclaimed to the counter-revolutionary crusaders: "In this sign shalt thou conquer!" From that moment, as soon as one of the numerous parties which had gathered under this sign against the June insurgents seeks to hold the revolutionary battlefield in its own class interest, it goes down before the cry: "property, religion, family, order." Society is saved just as often as the circle of its rulers contracts, as a more exclusive interest is maintained against a wider one. Every demand of the simplest bourgeois financial reform, of the most ordinary liberalism, of the most formal republicanism, of the most shallow democracy, is simultaneously castigated as an "attempt on society" and stigmatized as "Socialism." And, finally, the high priests of "religion and order" themselves are driven with kicks from their Pythian tripods, hauled out of their beds in the darkness of the night, put into prison vans, thrown into dungeons or sent into exile; their temple is razed to the ground, their mouths are sealed, their pens are broken, their law torn to pieces in the name of religion, of property, of the family, of order. Bourgeois fanatics for order are shot down on their balconies by mobs of drunken soldiers, their domestic sanctuaries profaned, their houses bombarded for amusement—in the name of property, of the family, of religion and of order. Finally the scum of bourgeois society forms the *holy Phalanx of order* and the hero Crapulinski installs himself in the Tuileries as the *"saviour of society."* (*EB*, pp. 20–21)

The very motion of events described in such a passage is conceived only in relation to a point of present time always already contained in the master narrative of property, family, religion, and order. This is, in precise terms, far from being the conventional journalistic practice of a style that expresses contempt or sorrow for what is at the same time recognized as the inherent logic of the world. As dependent as the *Eighteenth Brumaire* is upon a broad intertext of secular and biblical classicism, this dependence is not stylistic but critical in nature. The literary orchestration of Marx's discourse marks the real, social power of Tradition, its influence in determining even the formal possibility of actuality. Since history itself does not move except in the shape of Tradition, of the already given, it is this Tradition itself that must supply the units in which to clock and measure historical motion. What modernism must reject—or find ways of rationalizing—as a crippling dependence on master narratives of the premodern (even if the *Eighteenth Brumaire* does work out of a partially critical consciousness of certain of these narratives) is precisely that which supplies the text with a critical-theoretical platform.

The real ideological stamp of modernism is to be detected in precisely this spontaneous disposition to read these and other similar passages in the *Eighteenth Brumaire* as so many stylistic tours de force in which the discursive figure of inversion stands for what is finally no more than a representational falsehood. Repetition is read by modernism as simply the apparent form of a history that drags its conventional and political representations behind it in the wake of its modern excesses of complexity and abstraction. But if history itself has falsified the representational identities of politics, what then enables it to coincide with the object of a "negative," nonrepresentational cognition? How can that which is figured negatively in a modernist aesthetic be claimed as the essence of history and not simply a more "modernized" representation of it? What I have already described as the hypostasis and recuperation of the spectatorial subject enters here as the effective hypostatization of the cognitive immediacy implicit in the very concept of representation. History must be shown to repudiate its more obvious political fakeries in order that the already ahistoricized subject, whose self-identity is threatened by this process, may ultimately be saved from history. Modernism feeds on what is really, after all, the most conventional, and ideological, of historical representations: that of a historical past that does not trouble the subjective immediacy and self-identity of the present from which it is serenely—or tragically—contemplated.

But it is just where our modernist thinking reinvents the hypostatic time-space of a representational identity, just where modernism thinks it has placed a maximal distance between its own present and the past, that a critical concept of history makes its concealed entrance in the *Eighteenth Brumaire*. It is in the absence of *history* as a representational identity—in the farcical space of repetition where "words go beyond content"—that history concretely manifests itself by *withholding* the representational mechanisms of its self-identity as "present." History as an already stable object of meaning and activity—history as "made"—can be preserved only at the cost of its interminable repetition; it is only by reproducing the past that the representational identity of subject and object—of "people" and parliament, legislature and executive, smallholding peasant and *idée napoléonienne*—is affirmed. Tradition itself steps out of the past and usurps the contemporaneity that forms the ground of all conscious and "meaningful" self-activity. Tradition, or the "given circumstances," confers on events not merely the historical disguises in which to cloak their authentic content but also, and in a much more powerful maneuver, their meaning as "events," the sense that, in them, anything has happened at all. Marx's continual recourse to the classically ironic figure of inversion, although legitimately read as a stylistic device, can also therefore be read as consistent with the critique of a historically determined form of false consciousness.

X. "A State That No Longer Represents Anything"

Let me attempt now to reconstruct *this* particular historical determination, working out of Marx's text as well as out of his general line of social critique. My lateral aim shall be to show how modernism, by rewriting the *Eighteenth Brumaire* in terms of an aesthetic crisis in representation, itself assumes a reifying relation to that crisis.

I begin by observing that the question of a crisis in representation arises in the *Eighteenth Brumaire*, as generally in Marx's "political" writings, in reference to the question of *power*. Marx's self-proclaimed intent in the *Eighteenth Brumaire* is to explain "how the *class struggle* in France created circumstances and relationships that made it possible for a grotesque and mediocre personality to play a hero's part" (*EB*, p. 4). How, asks Marx, is something that from the outset is considered by bourgeois society to be a mere instrument of its political will, lacking any inherent authority—Louis Bonaparte, that is—able to convert itself into the power over bourgeois society itself? A theory of *political* representation based on the identity of an economic interest with a given instance of state power is rendered false by the coup d'état of 2 December 1851. " . . . The immediate and palpable result" of this event, writes Marx.

> was the victory of Bonaparte over the parliament, of the executive power over the legislative, of force without words over the force of words. In parliament the nation made its general will the law, that is, it made the law of the ruling class its general will. Before the executive power it renounces all will of its own and submits to the superior command of an alien will, to authority. The executive power, in contrast to the legislative power, expresses the heteronomy of a nation, in contrast to its autonomy. France, therefore, seems to have escaped the despotism of a class only to fall back beneath the despotism of an individual, and, what is more, beneath the authority of an individual without authority. The struggle seems to be settled in such a way that all classes, equally impotent and mute, fall on their knees before the rifle but. (*EB*, p. 122)

The explanation of this apparent reversal is assembled on two levels. In an immediate sense Bonaparte's triumph of 2 December is referred to his election as president on 10 December 1848 thanks to a massive peasant vote in his favor. Bonaparte is able to tame the power of both his left-wing and right-wing opponents through his ability to manipulate the mass of the peasantry with *ideés napoléoniennes* and their nostalgic promise of a return to the First Empire heyday of the smallholding peasant. Bonaparte "represents" the smallholding peasantry but only, as Marx reminds us, because and insofar as "they cannot represent themselves" (*EB*, p. 126).

But in representing the subjectless mass of the French peasantry, Bonaparte nevertheless attacks their material interests as a class through policies, such as excessive taxation, that drive them further and further into debt bondage. In this he continues to "represent" the material interests of the bourgeoisie, despite his suppression of bourgeois political liberties and privileges. It is here that Marx must resort to the explanation of the actual power of the Bonapartist state as, paradoxically, a *negation* of the very political forms in which the economically dominant class had given representation to its interests. The farcical and self-annihilating activity of the dominant bourgeois factions coalesced in the "Party of Order" only proves "the political rule of the bourgeoisie to be incompatible with the safety and existence of the bourgeoisie" (*EB*, p. 107), that the bourgeoisie "longed to get rid of its own political rule in order to get rid of the troubles and dangers of ruling" (*EB*, p. 107), and again that "the struggle to maintain its *public* interests, its own *class interests*, its *political power*, only troubled and upset it, as it was a disturbance of private business" (*EB*, p. 105).

There is clearly a degree of truth to the charges[17] that Marx here finds himself in the conceptually embarrassing position of having to emend his theory of power in post-1848 bourgeois society by essentially abandoning the notion of *class* as identical in all its representations. For Jeffrey Mehlman, in *Revolution and Repetition*, this evinces Marx's implicit abandonment of the philosopheme of representation altogether in favor of a theory of the state as pure "opposition" to society. And "what," asks Mehlman, "is the status of a State that no longer represents anything?"[18] Marx qualifies the apparent independence of the state from any given class interest by observing its representative relation to the mass of the French peasantry. But we have already seen that this relation is made possible only by the fact that the *Parzellen* do not themselves constitute a class, in the sense that their "identity of . . . interests begets no community, no national bond and no political organization among them" (*EB*, p. 126). The smallholding peasantry is, in other words, a class "in itself" but not "for itself"; it does not bear the attributes of a *class subject*. It is the Bonapartist regime that acts as the "for itself," as the subjectivity absent from the "uniform mass." And yet, at the same time that it acts *for* for this mass, it acts *against* its interest as defined in the impetus of the *Parzelle* to free itself of debt bondage. It is still the case that the identity of political will violates and contradicts the identity of economic interest.

More, however, can be inferred about the nature of this "independent" state than its apparent refusal of any class essence. It continues, in Marx's estimation, to safeguard an interest that, if it does not bear the consciousness of its class identity, nevertheless possesses a very real existence of its own. In the terminology of the *Eighteenth Brumaire* this is the "material power" (*materielle Macht*) of the middle class—a power that Bonaparte "protects" in the very process of breaking the "political and literary power" of the same class. "By protecting its [the bourgeoisie's] material power he regenerates its political power. The cause must accordingly be kept alive; but the effect, where it manifests itself, must be done away with" (*EB*, p. 135). In this still somewhat cryptic wording, Marx refers to the object of the greater part of his critical thinking subsequent to the *Eighteenth Brumaire*—to *capital as such*, divested of its powerful ideological representations and pseudotheorizations. A materialist interpretation of the *Eighteenth Brumaire* stands or falls on this point. If the Bonapartist state erects itself as power that is finally independent of the conflicting class interests that it mediates, it is because the very nature of its power is derived not from social relations expressed and contained in the domain of the "political" but from the precise social being of capital as a power over society and in "opposition" to it. Thus it is true that the theory of political power with which Marx initially operates in the *Eighteenth Brumaire*, and which is based on the identity of a class throughout its "political" and "economic" representations, eventually founders on the historical intrusion of a "material" class interest that is outside political representationality. However, it is not the premise of a representational identity per se that suffers this breakdown but rather the *specific representational forms in which power is given*. These forms—historically evolved and not the result of a philosophical deduction—prohibit the conceptual representation of a power that is at the same time abstract, or independent of the concrete individuals or class in whom power is thought to reside, *and* the bearer of the attributes of a real subject in the actual exercise of power.

The representationality of bourgeois revolution, in other words, fails to incorporate the representationality of capital. It is this crisis in representation—in inverted and ideologized form—upon which, in the terms of the genealogy I am attempting to assemble, modernism erects itself.

Thus I specifically attribute to the *Eighteenth Brumaire* the implicit but unarticulated postulate of a historically evolved instance of social power—capital—that, having required the political instrument of bourgeois revolution to catapult it into its position of social dominance, in effect supplants and turns against this instrument once it has been so posited. The particular and paradoxical effect of this inversion is to falsify theoretically the very political power by means of which capital, in practice, achieves its decisive victory over its various social obstacles. Capital as it appears or as it is represented in the consciousness of those social agents with whom it is synonymous in the sense of a political project of "revolution" is thus completely negated by really existing capital once its own revolution becomes an established fact. This explains why the state power erected in the process of bourgeois revolution as the "natural" and rational expression of bourgeois class interest is no sooner consolidated than it slips from the hands of the capitalists as an instrument of their combined social will and commences to operate "independently," as if it were not, strictly speaking, a political power at all but a kind of social automaton. The conceptual distinction between capital as economic interest and the state as its instrument and safeguard inevitably breaks down as the material power of capital acquires a political will of its own.

XI. Capital and Social Agency

The general slowness of Marxism in most, if not all, of its existing "currents" to articulate this ellipsis in the political representation of capital is perhaps best explained by the fact that Marx himself produces the theoretical concept of capital with almost exclusive reference to *labor*, a concept that, for what are undoubtedly complex historical reasons, remains largely outside the immediate conceptual domain of the political. Labor, as abstracted conceptually for the theoretical purposes of *Capital*, appears somehow foreign to the concept of power that premises Marxian theories of the state. The persistence of this conceptual split within Marxist thinking, though impossible to criticize adequately in the present context, need not, however, stand in the way of a political reading of precisely those areas in Marxian analysis in which the *Eighteenth Brumaire*'s "missing" concept is clearly articulated. For example, in the fourth notebook of the *Grundrisse* (the "Chapter on Capital," in the Nicolaus translation) Marx makes the following parenthetical comments:

> *Capital in general*, as distinct from the particular capitals, does indeed appear (1) *only as an abstraction*; not an arbitrary abstraction, but an abstraction which grasps the specific characteristics which distinguish capital from all other forms of wealth — or modes in which (social) production develops . . . ; (2) however, capital in general, as distinct from the particular real capitals, is itself a *real* existence.
> While the general is therefore on the one hand only a mental mark of the distinction [*differentia specifica*], it is at the same time a *particular* real form alongside the form of the particular and the individual.[19]

Capital's peculiar ontological status as a *real* abstraction is to be explained by the fact that in it are presupposed not only the concepts of all its particular manifestations — for example, ground rent, money, "fixed capital" — but also the very "objective conditions of living labour capacity" itself. These "objective conditions" are "presupposed as having an existence independent [of living labor capacity], as the objectivity of a *subject* distinct from living labour capacity and standing *independently* over against it" (*G*, p. 462; my emphasis). "Capital . . . is the existence of social labour—the combination of labour as subject as well as object—but this existence as itself existing independently opposite its real moments—hence itself a particular existence apart from them" (*G*, p. 471). "Abstraction" here carries the sense of a process in which society as subject is not only forced to apprehend the objective preconditons of its existence as an abstract contingency outside itself but of a process in which social subjectivity as the *actual locus of agency* ceases altogether to reside in the concrete individual or social group and pertains, instead, exclusively to capital. Capital, therefore, "acts" in the sense of a human subject but does so in a manner that can only be regarded as abstract from the point of view of "human activity" itself. Capital, in its generalized form as a social power, does not, in other words, merely resemble social agency in formal terms; it *is* this agency in abstract form, and its full-fledged existence is tantamount to the ultimate falsification of all "human" representations of agency or "autonomy" in the face of the historical process.

It is therefore the real, historical being of capital that explains the anomaly of a state that "no longer represents anything," not because representation as philosopheme has been falsified but because a particular and historically evolved form of social subjectivity has literally ceased to constitute the locus of agency. Likewise with the History "represented" in the actions of human protagonists— such a History loses its capacity to be given as a *present* because the real present in which "men make their own history" exists at the level of society as a whole only for a real, inhuman abstraction. Again from the *Grundrisse*,

> Once production founded on capital is presupposed . . . [then] the
> condition that the capitalist, in order to posit himself as capital, must
> bring values into circulation which he created with his own labour . . .
> belongs among the antediluvian conditions of capital, belongs to its
> *historic presuppositions* which, precisely as such *historic*
> presuppositions, are past and gone, and hence belong to the *history of
> its formation*, but in no way to its *contemporary* history." (*G*, p. 459)

It is this historic *disjuncture* which writes itself in the *Eighteenth Brumaire*, but only as it is implied for a purview precisely that of the "historic presuppositions" that are already "past and gone." It must therefore take the contemporary form of a repetition. Capital in the *Eighteenth Brumaire* manifests itself not as concept but rather as the unnamed and absent source of a narrative in which the representational identities of politics collapse in the farce of counterrevolution.

The point that must be constantly reaffirmed in all this—because of the constant danger that it will itself fall victim to its own inversion effect—is the preeminent and radical *historicity* and *materiality* of capital as real abstraction. The development of capital as a self-positing entity is directly encountered in the labor process itself, whose "automatic" functioning becomes, according to Sohn-Rethel, the chief postulate of capitalism as a "social synthesis": "From the perspective of the capitalist entrepreneur the essential characteristic of the production process is that it must operate itself. The controlling power of the capitalist hinges on this postulate of the self-acting or 'automatic' character of the labor process of production."[20] The crisis brought on by this development, however it is that "men become conscious of it," registers its prior effect as the *real loss* of a social autonomy previously exercised by, and identified with, human subjects, even if only by some and not others. The "subject of history" does not dissolve as if it had always been a simple illusion—rather, it comes to coincide on the plane of the material itself with the abstract social synthesis operated by capital. To the extent that they function reproductively within this social synthesis, human individuals must inevitably experience their own subjective activity as a representational falsehood; what would be their real activity as social subjects is preempted at the level of society as a whole. Society itself moves outside the space of subjective self-identity, making it impossible for what Marx and Engels in *The German Ideology* call "self-activity"[21] to itself be anything more than an abstraction, "incommensurable" with the real actions of human beings. Human actions take on social content only as aspects and fragments of a motion with an external and independent source, much as the labor power of the individual or collective laborer in the flow production process more and more relinquishes its subjectivity to the motive force of the production mechanism itself. The inevitable falsity of attempts to confer a quality of philosophically pure autonomy on the socially synthetic actions of human agents under the specific form of capitalist domination for which Marx reserves the term "mode of production" results directly from a historically given property of capital as a "particular and real existence" and not, as the idealized and hypostasized consciousness of crisis would tend to make us believe, out of some ultimate fallacy of representation. Any real transcendence of the crisis in representation brought on by capital would be possible only as that theoretical and practical critique that is itself premised on the real and historical nature of the crisis.

XII. Art as communal property

My examination of the specific intertextual field defined by the *Eighteenth Brumaire* and modernist aesthetic theory as propounded by Adorno may now perhaps be permitted to conclude in the observance of a final polarity. As I have gone to some lengths to demonstrate, the concept of negation upon which Critical Theory, following Adorno, bases its radical social defense of modern art contains an implicit refusal of revolutionary politics, which in its turn is made out to be the result of the late capitalist reification of all representational thinking. Fascism in particular appears to confirm the falsity of a *politics* of liberation by its insidious capacity to manipulate the proletariat through the use of the very representational devices (slogans, narratives, symbols, and such) in which the proletariat's self-identity as agent of revolution had once seemed secure. What is to be inferred from this, therefore, is the uncompromising necessity of preserving a critical stance toward the "administered universe" through a medium that by its very nature disclaims all representational truth. For if even the concepts through which a conscious negation of the present system is expressed are unsafe, negation must then also become the negation of its own conceptual medium. This new immediacy can be only the absolutely concrete, but representationally abstract, matter of art. Apart from its misplaced and "nineteenth-century" antiquarian faith in proletarian heroics, the *Eighteenth Brumaire*, in its prophetic grappling with Bonapartist fascism, may be cited as a cryptic index for just this radical turn to art. Implied in the language of tragedy and farce would seem to be already the notion of an essentially aesthetic mode of negation.

My alternative reading of Marx's text counters this aesthetic genealogy with the thesis of a crisis in representation that is a specific effect of the modern capitalist production process on the relations and discourses of power and agency. Capital itself, according to my theoretical sketch drawn from the *Grundrisse*, creates the necessity for a break between revolutionary praxis and the representational politics through which it has acquired an initial self-consciousness. Representation in this context cannot be severed from its political medium. Simply to propose the negation of this political medium through the agency of some extra-representational consciousness is to advocate metaphysics. Regaining the level of the concrete, of the "content that goes beyond the words," can be the outcome only of the real historical negation of the real and particular abstraction that is capital. What, to modernism, appears as the *Eighteenth Brumaire*'s contamination with the ideological master narratives of an outmoded and premodern political utopia, becomes, in light of this reading, a precise, if only seimarticulated registry of self-positing capital on the level of its narrative effects for a form of historical false consciousness. In its specific, and perhaps constitutive, incapacity to formulate itself as a critique of capital as real abstraction, Adornian modernism necessarily consigns itself to a position of radical idealism.

In order to clarify this final point, let us consider once again the powerfully modernist slogan pronounced by Adorno in fragment 94 of *Minima Moralia*: "Total unfreedom can be recognized, but not represented." If "total unfreedom" is interpreted in its real historical particularity as the capital that commands the labor production process, the affirmation of its nonrepresentability suggests nothing beyond the axiomatic truth that capital as abstract social subject is always nonidentical with its representations. The derivation of a synthetic meaning from Adorno's predication would require us to posit—in its absence—

the ideal subjective consciousness of a "freedom" endowed with its own conceptual presence. Expressed in the theory of capital as an abstract, suprapolitical power (a power that comes to explode and negate its own political armatures) is, however, *already* the loss of that which supplies the real, historical content of "freedom" as concept. Marx refers to this lost factor continually throughout the fourth and fifth notebooks of the *Grundrisse* as the essence of the various forms of *communal property*. "*Property* originally means no more than a human being's relation to his natural conditions of production as belonging to him, as his, as *presupposed* along with *his own being*; relations to them as *natural presuppositions* of his self, which only form, so to speak, his extended body" (*G*, p. 491). In the historical transition from commune (the term by which Marx refers to certain dominant aspects of all precapitalist relations) to capital, which is equivalent to the alienation of "property" as described above, there is indeed registered the loss of representation as an inherently subjective power—its reification—but this power *has no conscious reality distinct from the communal relation itself*. The subjective experience of freedom invoked by Adorno as a utopian state of consciousness, and which would make of "freedom" a kind of conceptual property, has no historical truth apart from the already socially mediated consciousness given directly in the lived bodily experience of the commune. Implicit in Adorno's utopian concept of representation as the ideal subjective appropriation of the world is a historical subject whose real social and historical existence as communal coproprietor has been inverted and hypostasized. For Adorno, "freedom" must first be realized conceptually before it can be affirmed as an actual attribute of society. But the inverse is what holds true: it is only with the real loss of "freedom" in the destruction of the communal property relation, that the concept itself arises—bearing, as a result of this genealogical inversion, all the features of ideology.

The efforts of theory to restore the already ideologized category of communal appropriation to a position of power—or, at least, of critical negativity—through the positing of a minimal and antirepresentational consciousness ("recognition") thus really accomplish nothing but the conveyance of ideology into the pseudomaterial dimension already waiting for it in the category of the *aesthetic*. In the Adornian conception of the modern work of art as the unique possibility of an unreified consciousness—which, *ipso facto*, makes it the uniquely possible instance of revolutionary agency—there is to be recorded nothing but the exclusively theoretical salvation from what is already a purely theoretical dystopia. It is thus not so surprising, given this ideological redoubling, if modern art, in the process of its theoretical defense, should begin to resemble what it negates only on the plane of ideology. Simultaneously concrete and abstract, subjective and nonhuman, autonomous but non-self-identical—is this not the utopianization of capital itself—a capital that has done away with its own social conditions of existence and with them the reality of "unfreedom"? Instead of an aesthetic posited on the affirmation of the communal property as something subjective, as a form of social existence whose negation by capital reveals, in this very process, the historical contingencies and contradictions inherent in the dominant power, modernism posits the aesthetic as a purely idealized instance of negation. But such negation, given the existence of capitalism, can be affirmed only as something existing asocially, as capital without its social relations—as if capital could negate itself and somehow emerge as something other than capital all over again.

Chapter 2
Modernism, Manet, and the
Maximilian: Executing Negation

I. Manet via Bataille: "To Suppress and Destroy the Subject"

On 19 June 1867, Emperor Maximilian I, Napoleon III's Hapsburg satrap in Mexico, was executed by troops of the Juarista army in the central Mexican city of Querétaro. The same date appears inscribed below the artist's signature in the best known of various canvases depicting the event that were painted by Edouard Manet and conventionally titled *The Execution of Maximilian*. The execution, about which Marx apparently never wrote but which has all the tragifarcical qualities of a page out of the *Eighteenth Brumaire*, has over the years generated a sort of subtradition of sentimental and popular narrative, which includes *corridos*, folk legends, historical novels, plays, an epic poem, and even a Hollywood film.[1] Manet's series of representations of the event, which include four oils and a lithograph, might also be counted within this subtradition were it not for the preemptive interference of a much more highly sanctioned claim laid upon these works by the tradition of orthodox high modernism. Thanks to this tradition the *Maximilian* now typically numbers as one of the various works by Manet (along with *La musique aux Tuileries*, *Le déjeuner sur l'herbe*, *Olympia*, and *Un bar aux Folies-Bergère*) that nearly every art history student is taught to recognize as the pathbreakers of modern painting in France and Europe generally. In Mexico the event itself retains a strongly symbolic cultural and political connotation, but outside Mexico one might almost speak of the event of Manet's painting as having displaced and supplanted the spectacle of the execution proper.

In his textual accompaniment to the Skira volume on Manet, Georges Bataille

Edouard Manet, *The Execution of Maximilian*, 1868. Courtesy Städtische Kunsthalle, Mannheim.

has written what is perhaps the epitome of a modernist interpretation of the *Maximilian*.[2] Repeating in stylized format Malraux's formalist interpretation (which itself originates with Zola),[3] Bataille sees in the *Maximilian* the enactment of a definitive and revolutionary "destruction of the subject." "Here Manet wrung the last drop of meaning out of the subject. To suppress and destroy the subject is exactly what modern painting does" (*M*, p. 48). To argue for this revolution, Bataille invokes the standard comparison of the Manet painting with Goya's *Shootings of May Third*. Manet's *Maximilian* is, according to Malraux (Bataille's principal authority), "Goya's *Shootings of May Third* minus what the latter picture signifies" (qtd. in *M*, p. 45). What in Goya's picture is an intensely emotional involvement in the subject has, in Manet's, become an absence, a quality of sheer "indifference." "In [the *Maximilian*] Manet paid scrupulous attention to detail, but even this is negative, and the picture as a whole is the negation of eloquence; it is the negation of that kind of painting which, like language, expresses sentiments and relates anecdotes" (*M*, p. 48).[4]

Bataille's strongly metaphysical investment in the category of negation, as manifest in these and other passages, has obviously strong affinities for the Adornian aesthetic, which I examined in Chapter 1. I shall add here only that Malraux, for Bataille, *is* Critical Theory "minus what it signifies" in the way of an explicit critique of capitalism. But on this interpretive plane the matter of influence is of scant importance next to the particular demonstration afforded by Bataille of how a metaphysics of social agency has become conceptually crucial to the interpretation of a given aesthetic artifact. For what makes the difference between Goya's painting and Manet's is thus not the historical referent itself: the experience of death before a firing squad is assumed to remain identical through time. The power to "negate" belongs to the *artwork* and determines a relation that is purely unmediated by "all values foreign to painting." The once great, but now degenerated, tradition of historical painting makes, according to modernism, its last appearance in this painting—but already as something no longer self-identical, as "negation." *"The Execution of Maximilian*—negatively speaking—represents a full world, free of the insipid comedies, the dust and litter of the past" (*M*, p. 50). *Seeing* the difference that Bataille sees (through the eyes of Malraux) thus presupposes the operation of that peculiar ideological effect of modernism that places art in the narrative cockpit of the revolutionary class. Indeed, if the Adornian *Eighteenth Brumaire* were to be magically transformed into a modernist painting, it might look like *The Execution of Maximilian*.

To be sure, there can be little doubt that the modernist interpretation of the *Maximilian* as a modernized, negative *Shootings of May Third* rests on solid iconographic ground. In making use of this highly charged comparison, however, Manet's modernist interpreters have in effect invented a pretext for suppressing another, no less observable, iconic genealogy that does not lend itself so easily to the identification of the painting as a work of proto-modernism. This "secondary" genealogy concerns both the way in which Manet's subject, however "negative," is initially selected and the preexisting encodement in which it became available for selection.

Let us pursue this "lost lineage." In a study published in 1954, Manet's Swedish critic and iconographer, Nils Sandblad, assembles extensive documentation of the nonpainterly sources on which, according to his detailed iconographic reconstruction of the entire *Maximilian* series, Manet must necessarily have relied.[5] The most important of these are the series of articles, often accompanied by lithographic illustrations, on both the progress of the Mexican civil war and the execution itself that were published in the Parisian newspapers, especially the *Memorial Diplomatique*, the *Moniteur*, and *L'Illustration*. Sandblad records the considerable interest evinced in the French, European, and North American reading publics generally over the "fate" of Maximilian after his capture by the anticolonial forces. When news of the 19 June execution finally reached France on 30 June 1867, having made its way via the United States and Austria across the transatlantic cable, it had acquired all the impact of an eagerly and tensely awaited climax to a serialized melodrama. After an apparently very short period of public waivering, blame for the *Mexicanische Kaisertragödie* (as it was labeled in Maximilian's native Austria) was laid squarely on the shoulders of the Second Empire and Napoleon III, prompting a political scandal for the Bonapartist regime.

Manet, according to Sandblad's reconstruction, began work on the first version of the *Maximilian* almost immediately after news of the execution had arrived in Paris. Four other versions, three more oils and a lithograph, were to follow without appreciable interruption. The five versions show a number of fairly discrete variations: the sombrero-ed and conventionally "Mexican" garb of the firing squad as it appears in the first, or Boston, canvas is replaced by regulation French uniforms in all subsequent versions; and the vague and open-air backdrop in the Boston and London versions changes to a plain stone wall showing "Mexican" spectators peering over its upper edge in the Copenhagen and Mannheim paintings. In contrast to the modernist, as well as to earlier realist and naturalist tendencies to read in these variations the signs of Manet's increasing "indifference" to the details of the execution and his primary concern for the manipulation of visual forms, Sandblad's reading of the series of press reports demonstrates a strict correspondence between the pictorial variations that Manet made and the accumulating and increasingly detailed information on the execution's physical setting that was becoming available to him. The only important exception to this textual correspondence is Manet's reported use of a squad of French *chasseurs à pied* from a nearby barracks as live models; Sandblad qualifies the "indifference" evident in the use of such models with a reference to a photograph of the real Mexican squad, showing them dressed in uniforms of a basically French type—a print of which was probably accessible to Manet at the time.

Having established this close, almost painstaking attempt at a quasi-literal reproduction of the execution as gleaned from a close reading of the news, Sandblad satisfies himself rather cheaply with the revelation of a Manet with more "human" qualities than those of the modernist "pure painter"—a Manet who, like the Picasso of *Guernica*, could pursue pure painting without having "given up [his] right to be effected by a Querétaro" (*MTS*, p. 161). Sandblad also basically concurs with each of the succesively dominant interpretations of the *Maximilian* (realist, naturalist, and modern) by refusing to grant more than peripheral importance to Manet's official disfavor under the Second Empire and the obvious potential for a critical retaliation in the treatment of his subject. The decision of the regime to intercede directly by prohibiting the lithographic reproduction of the *Maximilian* is simply noted as a biographical incident more or less in keeping with Manet's already established reputation as a "radical" in the eyes of the officials, a reputation that long denied him entrance to the Salon and kept his works from being exhibited in the Parisian *Exposition Universelle* of 1867.

[Manet's] sense of human pathos at a time when he considered himself the most persecuted of men drove him beyond the usual scope of his painting, and in his agitated condition of mind he allowed this to happen, although every newspaper reader in Paris would know how easily such a painting as this could be interpreted as an attack on Napoleon III. (*MTS*, p. 151)

But the theory that the *Maximilian* series represents really nothing more than a lapse into an older, increasingly discredited style of historical or narrative painting, permitted as a result of certain personal idiosyncrasies, is, like Bataille's more heroic theory of a conscious act of metarepresentational negation, premised on the idea of a History already available and transparent to representation. Regardless of its aesthetic propriety as "subject," History is simply *there* for the artist as an object awaiting his pleasure. But does not its simple presence as an object of representation, waiting to be affirmed or negated, imply that it is, at the same time, excluded from the present being of the artistic subject for whom it waits?

We have already seen how this spectatorial historicism emerges in Adornian modernism, as well as how the same optic functions dogmatically in Bataille's modernization of Manet. But even in the case of Sandblad's more empirically oriented interpretation this potent underlying mythology of the modern asserts itself undaunted in the face of iconographic evidence that reveals the precise way in which History departs from the preconceived forms of its objective self-identity and produces the very situation in which the artistic subject can contemplate its "absence." For what Manet paints in the *Maximilian* is not a negated History but a "mediatized" History, not an execution as execution but an execution as *news*.[6] Unlike the event portrayed in Goya's *Shootings of May Third*, Manet's subject is already given to representation as a mediated absence. The "event" of Maximilian's execution, as Manet and the mass reading public of which he is a part witness it, has all the properties that characterize a "negation of eloquence" *before* Manet appropriates it as the subject of an aesthetic intervention. If Bataille is right to insist on Goya as an implicit foil to Manet's representational practice, then it is a *historical* intervention—ignored by Bataille—that makes him right. Notions of "emotion" and "indifference" are ultimately superfluous in this context. It is Walter Benjamin who supplies the appropriate terms: in Goya, death before a firing squad is still linked to an *experience (Erfahrung)*; with Manet, it is becoming *information*.[7]

II. The Maximilian and the Media

Sandblad's scan of newspapers and periodicals reporting Maximilian's execution includes the following statement from the 3 July 1867 edition of the *Mémorial*

Diplomatique: "We will not be long in receiving details concerning this sad event, which, we are certain, will grant to the emperor Maximilian his true place in history") (qtd. in *MTS*, p. 109; my translation). It is, by Sandblad's calculation, during this initial stage of awaiting the "details" that Manet begins work on the Boston *Maximilian*. The Boston painting reproduces the few discrete facts at first known about the event after reports published in the same periodical on 10 August: Maximilian's Mexican attire (especially the sombrero) and the presence of the "sergeant" holding his musket at readiness for a coup de grace should the first volley of shots prove not to be fatal. Information not provided in the 10 August account—particularly the absence of a precise description of the physical setting of the execution, including the appearance of the firing squad—is reflected "negatively" in the painting's vague and undetailed backdrop and the "Mexican" dress of the soldiers, which Manet probably copied from earlier lithographic reproductions in *L'Illustration* depicting the battle of Jiquilpam in February 1865.[8]

This situation of waiting for additional information that is, somehow, *known in advance* to be in keeping with a certain "place in history" bears in a revealing way on Bataille's modernizing affirmation of "Meaninglessness" as the radically aesthetic effect of the "completed" painting—the Mannheim version. The event's mode of reception by a mass reading and viewing public shows that Manet, as a part of this public, relates to a "subject" that is, however, already "meaningless" in the special, circumstantial sense that it is *incomplete*— missing the "details"—as well as in the more general and qualitative sense of lacking a decisive narrative closure. The real complexity of this historical relation is totally passed over in Bataille's abruptly dogmatic invocation of a perfectly clean "negation" of a Goyaesque plenitudinous "meaning." The latter dialectic would assume a clean and unbroken passage of "meaning" from event to its mass reproduction that is finally "destroyed" only in the moment of its Manet-ian aesthetic representation. The moment of mass reproduction and reception is rendered entirely superfluous to interpretation. Quite a different result is derived, however, when the moment of mass *mediation* is accorded its own power of negativity. For despite the assurances of official authority in the *Mémorial Diplomatique*, there exists no spontaneous means of converting a fullness of detail into a narrative closure. Maximilian may indeed find "his true place in history" but only as a result of what must already strike the masses of readers as the emphatically anachronistic quality of his figure: a Hapsburg emperor in the age of the *Exposition Universelle*. Maximilian is *farce*; even his real death under unexpectedly "heroic" circumstances cannot produce the tragic "place in history" that his embarrassed backers desire for him—and for themselves. The accumulation of "facts" from the press accounts can only enrich—they can not alter—the semiotic incapacity of Maximilian to cease occupying what are, indeed, a multiplicity of "places in history." To modernize Maximilian by locating

him firmly in a self-identical contemporaneity is to rob him of the only meaningful presence he has, that of anachronism. To modernize Maximilian can, in
fact, only be to dissolve him in a particle wave of *information*—information that,
as a result of its social character as a negation of *Erfahrung*, loses, according to
Benjamin's analysis, its spontaneous embeddedness in a tradition.[9]

The traces of this same mass-mediatized and pre-aesthetic negativity are re-
plete in the tradition of submodernist narrative and pictorial representation al-
luded to above. In Zorrilla's quasi-epic poem *Drama del alma,* as well as in the
even more obscure "historical drama" written by the Austrian playwright Bie-
leck (*Mexico's letzter Kaiserzeit*), Maximilian takes on a Wagnerian Aura; anachronism purifies him of a contemporaneity that has become vulgar and mun-
dane. But these works themselves, if one bothers to read them, cannot fail to
leave an impression of extreme vulgarity—even of kitsch—resulting, ironically,
from poor Maximilian's failure to escape the vulgarizing taint of information,
even in the most elevated of discourses. Meanwhile, Maximilian, as a subject for
popular representation in the traditions of the *corrido* and of Mexican popular
graphic illustration and historirgraphy, exhibits the same tendency to dissolve into
a noncoherent mix of literary device and journalistic detail. The standard encodement presents "Maximiliano" and "the mad empress Carlota as narrative
counterfoils to the canonized figure of Juárez: the short, dark, full-blooded Indian patriot versus the tall, blond, blue-eyed imperialist usurper and devil. But
"Maximiliano" also undergoes a curious process of redemption and Mexican-
ization after his death and narrative reemergence as a cadaver. It is customary in
popular histories of Mexico to accompany the account of Maximilian's execution
with the evocative repetition of certain bizarre and macabre details: the emperor's
charro outfit, worn on the day of execution; his shout of "Viva México!" just
before the first volley of shots; difficulties in finding the proper materials for his
embalming, forcing the local undertakers to reconstruct his badly damaged face
with a pair of brown glass eyes plucked from a mannequin of the Virgin in a local
Querétaro church; and so on. The details of the event fail to produce the stable
effect of "meaning" prescribed by an official historical inscription, spilling over
the sharp edges of nationalist symbolism and blurring them in a carnivalized subplot out of *el día de los muertos.* Even the daguerreotype of Maximilian's corpse
on public display before the curious in a Querétaro cathedral shows him as a
rather swarthy, dark-haired figure, shorn of the insignia of his imperialist encodement.[10]

Were it not for the iconographic taboos of a modernist art historicism, Manet's
Maximilian series would fit easily into this peculiar subtradition. The "meaningless" effect produced by the unresolved conflict of two historical codes—the
informational/journalistic versus the traditional/experiential—is clearly visible as
the very process of variation and substitution that motivates the seriality. What
modernism will explain as a teleology of formal and "painterly" perfection—as

a "meaninglessness" endowed with closure and plenitude—can, on the contrary, be taken as an open-ended seriality in perpetual motion between the secured enclosures of a *Shootings of May Third* (or even of a Renaissance Crucifixion) and an actual photographic print of the 19 June execution—which, even if it does not exist, posits itself as something the public has the right to see. All the various "versions" of the painting, including the "definitive" (the Mannheim), would thus be interpreted as inherently unstable and *critical* (in the sense of *crisis*) representations that persistently transgress their modernist self-identities or frames. As *technique*, the *Maximilian* seriality would accordingly derive very little from its painterly medium—more from its lithographic—and would suggest, if anything, the principles of a "doctored" photograph or even a Heartfield photomontage. Bataille mistakenly identifies as a rejection of "all values foreign to painting" what may simply be—to again turn to Benjamin—the painterly discovery of a problematic of representation without a painterly solution.

But even the formal terms of traditional painterly criticism are sufficient basis on which to discover the real traces of critical representation in the *Maximilian*. Taking Goya's classic work and the general rules laid down since the Renaissance for the achievement of perspective and foregrounding in representations of the Crucifixion as indices of Manet's "debt" to Tradition, we can describe an inversion of traditional practice that is obviously more than a drive to formal abstractness. In Goya, as in the iconographics of a Crucifixion, a visual priority is accorded to the place of the victim; in the *Maximilian* this relation has been inverted, and priority is given to the group of executioners, who stand in the visual center of the frame at a point on a diagonal vector that brings them into more intimate contact with the viewer. Maximilian and his generals stand in a position more removed from that of traditional visual interest; the smoke from the discharging muskets as well as a seemingly only halfhearted adherence to the effects of perspective make them appear as less the subjects of the representation than as its semianonymous set pieces. (In the Boston painting the smoke has nearly obliterated the features of Maximilian and his fellow victims.) They are in the very process of disappearing—not as historical subjects, however, but as icons that stamp the framed image with the authoritative meaning of Tradition. In rendering them this way, Manet has simply reproduced them in their prior inversion as historical entities: as the details that serve to give a fullness to the news item that is already "shot through with explanation." Where Goya represents a violent death that takes on a meaning only within the narrative enclosure that begins and ends in the life of its collective and eponymous hero (the defenders of a traditional Spain against a Napoleonic "modernity"), Manet is faced with a violence that has preempted the lives of its victims in its importance and interest to the viewer. To the extent that the *Maximilian* can be termed a work of realism, its reality is not that of an allegorized Crucifixion but violence as such—violence as inherently "newsworthy," violence as *fetish*. To construct this undeniably "revolutionary" achievement as simply a traditional narrative "minus what it signifies" implies an accommodation of this reality as something naturally given. Manet can perhaps be interpreted as hesitant before this modern ideological temptation: a clear fascination with violent death must still at this stage cover itself with the alibi of a traditional master narrative, however farcical and vulgar. Modernism, as propounded by Bataille, shows no such hesitancy:

> On the face of it, death, coldly, methodically dealt out by a firing squad, precludes an indifferent treatment; such a subject is nothing if not charged with meaning for each one of us. But Manet approached it with an almost callous indifference that the spectator, surprisingly enough, shares to the full. *Maximilian* reminds us of a tooth deadened by novocaine; we get the impression of an all-engulfing numbness, as if a skillful practioner had radically cured painting of a centuries-old ailment: chronic eloquence. Manet posed some of his models in the attitude of dying, some in the attitude of killing, but all more or less casually, as if they were about to "buy a bunch of radishes." Every strain of eloquence, feigned or genuine, is done away with. There remain a variety of color patches and the impression that the subject ought to have induced an emotional reaction but has failed to do so — the curious impression of an absence. (*M*, p. 48)

Imagine the classic Vietnam war photographic image, the one that shows a Saigon police official executing a Vietcong suspect at close range, praised in this way. Even the most cynical of ideologues would disavow it. Such an aesthetic "distance" would violate the decorative journalistic concern for an overriding "human interest" — that high circumscribed area in which reporting has the license to give itself "literary" airs. The fact that Manet paints his subject — a subject whose objective existence as "news" is already dismissed in this interpretation[11] — nevertheless permits a modernist art criticism to do something exactly analogous without embarrassment. The day-to-day reality of political violence is now, to be sure, the practically unchallenged province of journalistic and documentary representation, except for those rare and usually well-hidden instances in which a collective experience successfully preempts the dominant overlays of information (for example, present-day Nicaragua) and reinvents the epical tradition of a Goya.

But with modernity firmly in control of its own mechanisms of naturalizing ideology, reencountering the kind of codal fissure traced in the *Maximilian* perhaps terminates the painterly gesture that it has innocently stumbled into and set in motion, in the manner of a *flâneur*, abandoning the field to the more modern representational techniques of lithography, photography, film, and video. And maybe that is the "negation" we should credit to Manet.

III. The Maximilian on The Barricade

When forced to allow for a residual content in Manet's painting, the modernist Bataille falls back into a curiously metaphysical vein and refers to its "theme" as the "idea of death." (*M*, p. 46). The idea of death is said to exert an "attraction" on Manet that leads him to revert to it in a series of works: *The Dead Toreador* (which actually predates the *Maximilian*), *The Funeral*, *The Suicide*, and the "street scenes" that Manet sketched during the days of the Paris Commune. All of these thematically interlocking works purportedly bear witness to Manet's "desire to subordinate—or sublimate—the horror of death in a naively unconcerned play of light." (*M*, p. 50). Such a "play of light" is in turn implied as the aesthetic equivalent of the historical transparency that characterizes Manet's quintessential subject as a painter: "a pure state of being." (*M*, p. 63). Modernism thus attributes to itself as something "stark" and "ruthless" the very same naive ontologism that underlies the quotidian matter-of-factness of journalistic representation. Manet's art has shown us a "supreme, unimpeachable reality" by simply painting "what was there." Never mind if Manet, like everyone else, had to read about "pure being" in the newspapers.

The recourse to a kind of catalog of universal "themes" betrays the reliance of modernizing interpretation on the narrative structures of a dominant ideology—the "transparency" and immediacy of information—of which modernism itself is a more complex discursive instance. The narrative of "eloquence" and "majesty" is supplanted by the narrative of simple *presence*, which, like all dominant ideologies, does not regard itself as a narrative at all. The neatness of this operation would be all but flawless in the case of the *Maximilian* series were it not for the fact that the thematics of "death" do not really make for a convincing explanation of the highly discrete and detailed variations that define the series. We have already noted the firing squad's change of uniform (indicating a possible change of nationality) and the addition of a more detailed background: mutations that, as Sandblad has shown, reproduce approximately the serial order of "facts" unveiled in the concurrent newspaper accounts. Are these then simply the result of a fascination with Death?

The improbability of such a theory is heightened even further by the existence of a lithographic print executed by Manet in 1871: entitled *The Barricade* (also the title of a watercolor version done in the same year), it features the same squad of French *chasseurs à pied* firing on a group of unarmed men with their backs to a barricaded street.[12] The spatial arrangement of the figures is fundamentally identical to that worked out in the *Maximilian* series. The squad now stands in the left foreground (still on the right in the original recto of the printing surface) and the sergeant cocking his musket for the coup de grace is missing. What we have is the *Execution of Maximilian* transposed to a Parisian boulevard. Maximilian and his two generals have fully confirmed the visual impression of their margin-

Edouard Manet, *The Barricade*, 1871. Courtesy Museum of Art, Rhode Island School of Design. Purchased and presented by Murray S. Danforth, Jr.

ality and interchangeability by shedding their identifying marks and assuming the new identity of Communards at the time of the recapturing of Paris by reactionary Versailles and Prussian troops. It is as if Manet had again endeavored to "paint the news" long after the Maximilian episode had subsided—although, according to his biographers, Manet expressed his sympathy for the Commune by remaining in Paris throughout its short life span and thus may have witnessed this particular, and surely less mediatized, news item firsthand.

Does not *The Barricade* show every formal sign of belonging to the *Maximilian* series? And why is Bataille unable or unconcerned to recognize this serial reprise except as a peripheral and effectively trivialized thematic reversion? Clearly, Bataille adheres, as would any orthodox art critic, to the standard identities of frame and time of execution. Manet's *work* on the *Maximilian* ends in 1868 with the completion of the definitive version now hanging in the Kunsthalle at Mannheim. *The Barricade* is sketched and lithographically recorded in 1871; it cannot be part of the *same* work without violating the principles of spatiotemporal identity required by interpretation. But here the logic is as rigorous as it is circular. Interpretation in effect discovers its "definitive" versions in just those locations that will assure it a definite interpretive outcome and protect it from others that are, a priori, dangerous or inadmissible.

Omission of *The Barricade* from the closed seriality of the *Maximilian* may seem, after all, to be a trivial instance of such interpretive maneuvers. But the effect of reading this work into the series opens up certain interpretive possibilities that further complicate the modernist claim on Manet. Using a Benjaminian aesthetic buttressed by Sandblad's iconography, I have already shown the possibility of explaining a painterly "indifference" and "meaninglessness" as the precise effects not, as modernism would have it, of an aesthetic manipulation but rather of a preexisting situation in which the demand for a traditional or experiential realism can realize itself only as an intermittent flow of information. The result is a representation that appears (to modernism) to repudiate its initial dependence on the "subject" even to the point of reversing the norms of traditional realism by reducing the status of the subject to that of a mere "pretext." But such an appearance can itself be explained as nothing more than an ideologically motivated *inversion* of a particular and real historical crisis in realism as a representational effect. By permitting *The Barricade* to augment the series, we add an even greater dimension of historicity to this de-aestheticizing of "indifference."

Although a greatly sensationalized "media event" in its own right, the execution of Maximilian in 1867 signified in highly melodramatic terms what was already an accomplished fact some months before: the failure of the French imperialist exploit in Mexico. Although of relatively little consequence to the economic strength of the Second Empire, it dealt a severe blow to the already weakened edifice of Bonapartist chauvinism. The apparent rapidity with which public opinion turned against Napoleon III, despite the imperious coachings of such official press organs as the *Memorial Diplomatique*, is not remarkable in itself, but it demonstrates the precarious hold of certain *idées napoléoniennes* on the masses whose successful manipulation was essential to the hegemony of the Bonapartist bloc. The spontaneous conversion of an official "tragedy" into a public farce posed no immediate threat to the bases of state power as such; it did, however, confirm a state of objective crisis in the populist ideological strategy of the dominant power. Though there is no historical evidence to suggest that a rival hegemonic discourse had yet succeeded in condensing their amorphous antagonisms, the masses perhaps did, for a time, cease behaving like properly Bonapartist subjects.

In the relation of the *Maximilian* to its "subject," which for Bataille and modernism becomes a purely cognitive negation arising from a state of aesthetic indifference, we may equally well detect the lack of ideological resolution expressed in the objective crisis of Bonapartist imperialism. This, however, becomes apparent only by inverting the conventional interpretive grammar that requires us to conceive the "subject" as exclusively *selected* by the aesthetic agency—be it "artwork" or "artist"—and by considering the manner in which the "subject," as a bearer of ideology, attempts to govern the circumstances under which it is 'selected." This initial prerogative of the "subject" shows itself clearly in the efforts of Bonapartist officialdom to assure the French public of what it already knows to be the "tragic" significance of the death of Maximilian. And it is unquestionably this preexisting ideological accent that *selects* the "aesthetic" selection of Manet by supplying him with his "subject." Modernism, of course, recoils at the thought that a "man of destiny" such as Manet should have his "autonomy" compromised in this way—but such a compromise could no more be evaded by Manet than it could by the rest of the French public of which, unless I am very mistaken, he was a part.

Official ideology, however, does not entirely succeed in salvaging its Mexican epic with a tragic epilogue. The tragedy fails to make its appearance, either out of the "blank slate" of mass opinion or out of Manet's palette and sketchbook. Its epic increasingly assumes the quality of a mock-epic, and its epilogue suggests a farce. As modernists, we resort to various kinds of historicizing and psychologistic mythology to explain what undeniably appears to be a critical rupture in representation, inventing, in the case of Manet and modern art generally, a supreme deus ex machina of conscious, critical negation. We forget that criticism itself, however free its exercise, has its historical premise in the objective reality of social *crisis*. Accordingly, we overlook the extent to which official ideology, in its failure as pre-selected "subject" to determine the precise mode of its representation, has entered into a state of chronic irresolution that does not immediately produce the effect of a clean, dialectical *Aufhebung*. We thus naturally refrain from explaining the "indifference" evident in Manet's treatment of his "subject"as itself a manifestation of prolonged ideological crisis. We correctly attribute to Manet's "play" on representational orthodoxy—its subtle violation of the traditional iconography of Crucifixion as well as its montagelike manipulation of certain crucial details—a degree of autonomy but rush to invert this critical opening by suspending it in an aesthetic theology. In actuality, though, Manet's "aesthetic" criticism, conditioned as it is by the prior "mediatization" of the "pure being" it evokes, goes as far as, and no further than, the then-existing crisis in official ideology as it expressed itself in a high degree of public skepticism and "indifference" falling far short of a revolutionary opposition or initiative.

To confirm this, we need look no further than to *The Barricade*. Here Manet returns to his "subject" but finds it, like its ideological donor, drastically changed. With the defeat of the French forces at Sedan and the subsequent revolutionary upheavals in Paris (the "Paris Revolution" of 4 September 1870, followed by the declaration of the Commune on 28 March 1871), the ruling Bonapartist bloc has "solved" its ideological crisis through its own objective collapse. After the retaking of the city by counterrevolutionary troops and the ensuing wholesale slaughter of the Commune, the "tragedy" of French imperialism can at last be represented in complete seriousness. The curious "detail" of the French uniforms now suddenly makes sense.

Does *The Barricade*, then, give us the *real* Manet, the radical painter of History, freed from the aestheticized torpors of the Second Empire? Is this the modernist, finally, as revolutionary? It is a tempting fantasy. *The Barricade* does indeed bear witness to a certain radical tradition in realism; however, it is not one that Manet initiates or invents, but one to which he returns. *The Barricade* realizes a specific closure of the *Maximilian* series—not through a conversion to the post-Bonapartist ideology of the Commune but by taking refuge in the pre-Bonapartist days of the Republic—by representing 1871 in the language of 1848.[13] For its middle-class supporters, the Commune was, in fact, imagined to be just such a return to radical Republican traditions. The hesitations and irresolutions of 1867 are rectified not, as modernism imagines, by the alchemical discovery of a transcendent *modernity* but by a radical repetition of 1848. With *The Barricade* we are back in the "June days," and the authoritative presence of Tradition—that of Goya but also of Meissonier, Adolphe Leleux, and Daumier—betokens itself in the appearance of its iconic centerpiece: the barricade itself.[14] To be sure, 1871 is both the source and receptacle of historical resonances that neither the imperialists nor the Communards are in any position to perceive fully. What issues from the defeat of the Commune is, in so many words, modern imperialism itself—an imperialism that has "cured" itself of Napoleonic infantilism. Lenin is the first to understand this and state it decisively. But there is a legitimate modernity too in Manet's reversion to the traditions of 1848, even if the discourse of aesthetics fails to recognize it: it is the deferred modernity of the *Eighteenth Brumaire*.

IV. Manet and the State: The Politics of Oil

For modernism, Manet is, above all else, a *painter*—that is, a skilled craftsman in the use of color. Based as it is on a certain degree of empirical truth, this somewhat dogmatic emphasis works well as an alibi for the omission of Manet's graphics and sketches when it is time to pronounce an authoritative interpretation. Thus the indirect political referentiality retroactively assumed by the *Maximilian* through its serial augmentation in *The Barricade* tends, at the outset, to be sidetracked if only because the lithograph remains outside the privileged space of *paint*. It is, to be sure, a matter of technical knowledge that the use of oils permits the artist to correct and add finish to the picture without abandoning the canvas, whereas the use of watercolors, lead and lithographic pencils, and engraving tools often requires the artist to "get it right" the first time. However, it is not merely technique but also a certain ideology that equates the high finish of oil with a quality of transcendent "finished-ness" over and against the casual "interest" implied in a mere sketch. We have seen that it is Manet's rapidly executed lithographic work *The Barricade* that, more than any other image, *defines* the *Maximilian* by enabling its serial displacements to come to rest in the provisional closure of Tradition. It is, in fact, the painted images that, from the standpoint of ideology, show the greatest degree of "unfinished-ness." By equating paint with closure, modernism more easily blinds itself to the submodernity of political narrative.

It would be mistaken, however, to suppose that modernism refrains entirely from political narrative in its invention of Manet as a modernist "revolutionary." It is customary knowledge that Manet—comrade, as he was, of Baudelaire—showed his contempt for official bourgeois taste in such notorious works as *Le déjeuner sur l'herbe* and the *Olympia* and was roundly attacked, as a result, by the art bureaucrats of the Second Empire. Despite Zola's consistent defense of Manet's work, Manet's official disfavor lingers on until late 1881—well after the fall of Napoleon III—when he is made a chevalier of the Légion d'Honneur thanks to his friend Antonin Proust, now minister of art. If, on the one hand, Manet's art remains "above politics" of the ordinary day-to-day sort, Manet—as an artist true to his mission—must nontheless engage the state in consistent battle in order to achieve a deserved public recognition. The acts of "violence" that give this "political" subplot its "revolutionary" flavor readily present themselves as the series of famous scandals provoked by the public exhibitions of *Le déjeuner sur l'herbe* in the Salon des Refusés of 1863 and of *Olympia* in the Salon of 1865. The anecdotal richness of these "outbursts of scorn and derision with which ever since the public has greeted each successive rejuvenation of beauty" (*M*, p. 16) emanates from these images as the aura of the avant-garde: the secure knowledge that by entering into a relation of affectionate and contemplative intimacy with these paintings, one puts an unbridgeable distance between one's self and the philistinism of the "crowd."

The *Execution of Maximilian* has, too, its story of scandal to tell. Manet, according to his biographers, had hoped to exhibit a number of his works, among them the *Maximilian* (probably the Boston or London canvas), at the *Exposition Universelle* in 1867 but was excluded and forced to rent space in the nearby Place de l'Alma for an unsanctioned showing. During that same year, Manet produced the lithographic version of the *Maximilian* and had gone so far as to send the stone to the printer when the government intervened by ordering the printer not to reproduce it. In subsequent years Manet was able to exhibit the *Maximilian* in New York and London, but as late as 1952, the year of Sandblad's monograph, and long after the important Manet exhibition in Paris in 1932, neither the lithograph nor any version of the painting had been publicly exhibited in France.

That this overt policy of censorship had a political motive that went beyond the defense of "public morals" — *Le déjeuner sur l'herbe* and *Olympia* principally were assailed by the critics and the "public" for sexual indecency — is a fact readily admitted by Manet's modernist critics. As a rule, however, it is dismissed as a circumstance extraneous to the aesthetic radicalism of the work as such and bearing witness merely to the caricatured philistinism of the Second Empire and Napoleon III. Sandblad cites a press notice, found among Manet's letters to Theodore Duret and probably written by Manet himself, that chides the government for refusing to permit reproduction of the lithograph, which, it is implied, was without political overtones: "We are amazed at this act of the authorities of slapping a ban on a purely artistic work" (qtd. in *MTS*, p. 155; my translation). Modernism generally repeats this defense, explaining the actions of the government as a mere instance of needless and puerile overreaction.

There is, however, a subtle ideological ruse at work in this gesture of exasperated dismissal. The state is made to appear infantile and almost innocuous when, in actuality, it had openly declared a very definite and serious *raison d'état*. For the state clearly did not intervene with its direct legal powers in order to suppress Manet's "aesthetic" activities (Manet was not fined or imprisoned or in any way prevented from carrying out his work as an artist) but to suppress the "public" itself by preemptively denying it access *as a mass* to the *Maximilian*. Such a mass access was possible only through the mass-mechanical reproduction of Manet's picture. For the lithograph, unlike an oil painting, was, according to Sandblad, "a work of art intended for a wide public, suitable for a topical subject, and which could have a political accent" (*MTS*, p. 153). The state understood this distinction, even if Manet did not, or pretended not to, and acted to suppress the topicality and "political accent" that would inevitably adhere to Manet's lithograph. It appears not to have acted, as modernism suggests, in mere conformity with the "reactionary" public but just as much in *conflict* with the public as a potentially antagonized agent of political interpretation.

Is it not more than purely fortuitous that the efforts of the state to restrict Manet to an "aesthetic" vocation with no direct contact with a mass public come here to coincide with the efforts of modernism to confer upon Manet the heroic task of "freeing" painting from the "reactionary" demands of official taste? Do not modernism and the state desire the same thing within the territories of their own prearranged spheres of discourse, and do they not share a concept of the "artist," even if the state derives this concept from a restrictive and limiting authority while modernism produces it out of a metanarrative of emancipation? Does not modernism simply legitimate as an instance of "aesthetic" freedom what the state has already established, by the use of its repressive power, as a limit on representational activity? Thinking as modernists, we parenthetically dismiss the censoring of Manet's lithograph with the rationale that, after all, the masses would not have "understood" it. But is this not already an inversion of historical reality? Can it not equally well be said that the evident failure of the public to "understand" the *Olympia*, and so forth, is already the *result* of a policy of censorhsip that has taken on the form of an artistic subjectivity and "autonomy" and that only confirms itself objectively in the attempt made to *transgress* its own limit in the lithographic conversion of the *Maximilian*? By inverting the order of determination as it really exists historically, by taking the practice of suppressing and restricting representational practice out of history and into the metaphysical space of aesthetics, does not modernism itself commence to operate as the ideology of censorship?

Chapter 3
Juan Rulfo: Modernism
as Cultural Agency

I. "Una Historia Imposible de Situar en Europa"

However we receive the appearance of the "postmodern" in contemporary metropolitan literary circles, there is at least one shared premise uniting the positions of those who sympathetically proclaim this current, those who have greeted it with skeptical annoyance, and even those prescient few already announcing its decline. This is that modernism itself, whether merely transfigured or defunct, no longer inspires any doubt as to its orthodox, canonical status. The least we can say of the postmodern is that it denotes a generation of authors for whom the once controversial figures of a Joyce, a Breton, or a Faulkner have acquired the aura of a classical tradition to be overthrown or sublated, as the case may be. Following certain critics who have designated a Beckett or Robbe-Grillet as already virtually postmodern, we could go even further in the adding of entries to our uniform literary genealogy. We are, at any rate, a far cry from the left debates of the 1920s and 1930s over modernism and realism. Rereading these polemics today, we must continually remind ourselves that the modernism opposed by Lukács and defended by Bloch, Adorno, and (although more ambivalently) Brecht was still not quite yet in its present position of cultural (post-) hegemony. The proliferation of critical works on modernism that propose to assess this movement as a whole—often as not in the past tense—corroborate an apparent intellectual consensus that modernism occupies a secure niche in our cultural heritage.

Turning to the present literary scene in Latin America, however, we see that the situation changes. There is, of course, an immediate philological distinction to be drawn between modernism as understood in the North American and European *ciudad letrada* and a *modernismo* that in Spanish America denotes a tradition, whose works are not, for this reason, any longer designated as "modern." Instead, this attribution tends to be made of a body of literary works that, although dating in some cases from as early as the 1920s, for the most part appear after the Second World War. The literature that lays the tacitly least controversial claim to modernity is that of the so-called *generación del boom*, a group of writers of narrative fiction mainly, of whom several are still active and in whose shadow much contemporary Latin-American writing continues to be produced. Many, if not most, of the names are familiar to the metropolitan reader from the dust jackets and reviews of their frequently best-selling works: Gabriel García Márquez, Jorge Luis Borges, Mario Vargas Llosa, Julio Cortázar.

The genealogy of this modernism is the subject of intense critical discussion and analysis. Early attempts to trace the new Latin-American literature to the influence of foreign models—in poetry, the surrealists; in prose fiction, that of Faulkner in particular—have, especially since the Cuban Revolution, tended to be de-emphasized in a more consciously nationalist or regionalist impetus to set forth the uniquely local sources of a literature that, if it does betray the superficial traits of outside influence, transforms the foreign element into a radically original compound. It is this complex, synthetic originality that, as this general line of thinking goes, lays proper claim to a modernity that would otherwise—if allowed to retain its privileged but alien metropolitan exemplarity—fall victim to its own intolerable unmodernity as a repetition.

There is every reason to prefer this regionalist and autonomizing construct of Latin-American modernity as a means of illuminating what might otherwise be distorted by the worst kind of mechanical, colonizing pseudoclassification. In bringing this seemingly dialectized genealogy to bear on the texts themselves, however, criticism does not automatically free itself of other, less obvious ideological burdens. In accordance with an overall critical conviction that the idea of modernity per se—however reduced in metropolitan parlance to the status of a historical artifact—conceals one of the most powerfully operant ideologies of present-day capitalist life, I shall attempt in this chapter to show how the interpretation and "modernization" of a specific Latin-American opus reproduce a number of discrete variations on the general ideological theme.

The work I shall consider here is that of the late Mexican author Juan Rulfo, consisting of the collection of short stories *El llano en llamas* (1953) and the novel *Pedro Páramo* (1955). It would doubtless be inaccurate to claim for these works the role of inaugurating single-handledly modern Latin-American fiction—as it would to credit any single work or author with that achievement. It can, however, be said without exaggeration that Rulfo's notoriously brief literary production—perhaps in part for the oracular impression left by its very brevity—

has come to occupy a rare position in modern Latin-American literary historiography,[1] particularly in the Mexican national tradition, wherein Rulfo's pathbreaking reputation is accepted wisdom. Although received somewhat skeptically upon its first publication,[2] *Pedro Páramo* was able, through good agencies of cultural *caudillos* such as Alfonso Reyes, Octavio Paz, and Carlos Fuentes, to ascend rapidly to classical and even legendary status. These latter two authorities in particular have contributed to the legend of a Rulfo who penetrated by sheer force of poiesis into the epical and even mythical unconscious of peasant Mexico.[3] Rulfo himself did little to hinder the production of this bardic aura, maintaining a spectacular public silence punctuated only infrequently by interviews and appearances on the international literary star circuit. Indeed, much of the critical interpretation of Rulfo has subtly succumbed to this type of auratic elevation by subjecting *El llano en llamas* and *Pedro Páramo* in particular to exhaustive myth-critical, linguistic, and structuralist analysis.[4] Meanwhile, a seemingly interminable series of reeditions, scores of scholarly articles, doctoral dissertation, and monographs, and inclusion in what must surely be as many university syllabi, attest to the continued iconizing of these two works, which, along with Paz's *El laberinto de la soledad*, are esteemed as the quintessential literature of modern Mexico.

Rulfo has had a similar success with a left-oriented criticism and intellectual opinion. One of the earliest indications of this is Carlos Blanco Aguinaga's influential article "Realidad y estilo de Juan Rulfo."[5] Blanco Aguinaga describes at length what, in a Marxist view of things, would be grounds for linking Rulfian narrative to the ideologies of bourgeois decadence: unmediated subjectivism, a cultic emphasis on the irrational, an abstract temporality drained of history, and so forth. "We find ourselves," writes this critic,

> within a world from within which every historical occurrence is received
> with a resigned silence as a law both mechanical and inevitable,
> although superficial and without transcendent importance. . . . Rulfo's
> reality at length flows into a what is in fact a world without history,
> without time, a dead world. (pp. 93, 101; my translation)

But the fundamental historical, class nexus toward which this typically Lukácsian process of detection seems to lead remains deferred. Instead, Blanco Aguinaga concludes with an apology for these very same narrative symptoms (which, it seems clear, retain their retrograde ideological character in the "classical" metropolitan conjuncture):

> Rulfo's short stories and novel match a contemporary mood of anguish
> well defined by Lukács and exemplified in many writers. But they are
> forthcoming within a concrete locality [*una tierra concreta*] in which
> the situation of the characters takes on a highly particular aspect
> because there weighs upon it a highly particular historical set of

conditions. It is thus that, however subjective Rulfo's vision, however impregnated his narratives with an appearance of irreality and remoteness, everything here becomes exemplary: a mode of access to a historical reality yet more real, pertaining to a most concrete moment of Mexican existence. (P. 113; my translation)

Blanco Aguinaga evokes here what has since become a familiar argument in Latin-American criticism, especially since the excitement over "magical realism" (*lo real maravilloso*) that greeted books like García Márquez's *Cien años de soledad* in the late 1960s and early 1970s. Reduced to its fundamental logical moves, the argument proceeds as follows: the familiar polemic within left criticism over the political character of avant-garde and antirealist tendencies in literature—in a word, over modernism—sheds its exclusive, either/or constraints in the case of Latin America, because modern Latin-American literature— exemplified in fictional works like *Pedro Páramo* and *Cien años de soledad*— exhibits only superficially antirealist features, which are, in fact, the objective reflections of a local reality exceeding the familiar, middle-class world of the great European nineteenth-century realists. Local, historical circumstances, it is implied, have generated the possibility of a literature that overcomes the traditional modernism/realism duality by effectively being both modernist and realist at once. Thus Blanco Aguinaga's defense of Rulfian irrealism amounts to the defense of the radical alterity and particularity of a set of circumstances and conditions (the favorite word is *lo concreto*) that are entirely extra-aesthetic and historical in nature. None of the typically metropolitan modernist propositions regarding aesthetic autonomy and "art for art's sake" are required here to make the case for a literature that, as it turns out, bears only a surface resemblance to the orthodox high modernism of the metropolis.

The origins of this line of thinking are diffuse. They could be found as far back as José Martí's critical writings—in particular the emblematic essay "Nuestra América"—in which something approaching this radical vision of *lo concreto* is intimated. A less precocious source, however, can be cited in Alejo Carpentier's original 1949 prologue to his novel *El reino de este mundo*. It is here that Carpentier, in defending his narrative method against the possible objections of both the metropolitan vanguard and the more pro-realist sentiments of a resurgent Latin-American anticolonialism, introduces the coinage *lo real maravilloso* into the Latin-American aesthetic and critical lexicon.[6] The prologue, more or less openly addressed to Carpentier's French surrealist associates, recounts the decisive impression made on the author by a voyage to Haiti in 1943.

After sensing the by no means fictional sorcery of the Haitian setting, after having discovered magical warnings in the red roads of the Central Plateau and having heard the drums of Petro and Rada, I was driven to compare the miraculous reality recently experienced to the tiresome pretensions of breathing life into the marvelous that have characterized certain European literatures in the last few years.[7]

There follows a scathing rejection (albeit still typically surrealist in tone) of these "European literatures" ("the dream-makers have become bureaucrats") on the grounds of the purely intellectual, privatized character of their search for what might, in Walter Benjamin's convenient phrase, be termed "profane illumination."[8]

> But they forget, after dressing up as cheap magicians, that the miraculous becomes unequivocally miraculous only when it arises from an unexpected alteration of reality (a miracle), from a privileged revelation of the real, from an illumination that is inhabitual or singularly favorable to the unnoticed riches of reality. ("P," p. 11; my translation)

This "privileged revelation" Carpentier claims to have found in Haitian *voudun*, a popular religious practice that becomes emblematic for him of Latin-American experience in general.

> But it occurred to me . . . that this presence and endurance of the miraculously real [*lo real maravilloso*] was not the unique privilege of Haiti but the patrimony of all of America, where there remains to be established, for example, a recounting of cosmogonies. ("P," p. 13; my translation)

El reino de este mundo, we are to understand, is itself nothing more than such a "recounting," in this case of the seemingly fantastic events making up the Haitian Revolution—"una historia," Carpentier adds, "imposible de situar en Europa" ("P," p. 15).

"A history impossible to situate in Europe": this, in a phrase, is the claim that Blanco Aguinaga makes for Rulfo's phantasmal novel *Pedro Páramo*. The apparent ahistoricity conveyed by Rulfian narrative is claimed to be merely an effect, generated by a habit of reading linked to conventional categories of historical narrative as deployed in European realism. Rulfian narrative opens onto a subject traditionally barred from participation in a dominant, rationalized version of History. If history as experienced by such a subject comes across as fundamentally static and given to irrational, even supernatural, occurrences, then this is to be explained precisely as an index of how radically disjunctive the two worlds— Europe and "América," metropolis and periphery—have been from the start.

That which is identified by the dominant, rationalizing, historicizing intellect (implicitly represented by Lukács in Blanco Aguinaga's essay), via a purely negative recognition, as the *irrational* belongs, in fact, to another neglected but wholly material sphere of life—that of *culture*. For the implication of Carpentier's prologue is that a true revelation of Latin-American historicity begins not on the level of diachrony as such—since this dimension is already initially claimed by the dominant historicity—but on the synchronic plane of a local cultural interpretation of historical events. Cultural difference marks a clear, unmistakable rift between the two worlds, whereas History, given its inherently universalizing and rationalizing concept, reduces difference, hence identity, to the point of dissappearance. The periphery does not share the privilege of the metropolis, for which History and Culture are ultimately one and the same thing, united in the grandiose category of "civilization." (Think of the immediately historical dimension called to mind when one speaks of European "culture.") Here culture is, on the contrary, the point of entry into a "a historical reality yet more real," which otherwise remains hidden from view. In proclaiming the cultural difference of "América" as the key to its historical identity, Carpentier, in effect, proclaims its *modernity* as both original and autonomous.

Blanco Aguinaga, and the left espousal of Rulfian narrative that has generally followed in the wake of his essay, repeats this operation by dismissing the superficially antirealist features of *El llano en llamas* and *Pedro Páramo* as being the price of a more deep-seated and radical *cultural realism*. Such cultural realism resides in Rulfo's supposed fidelity to the popular speech and oral narrative forms of his native region of Jalisco. "In effect, no one writes," claims Blanco Aguinaga; "someone speaks" (p. 110; my translation). In its more naive versions this idea has resulted in the image of Rulfo as a kind of ethnographic medium, a mere recorder and transmitter of a regional, oral tradition. Certain of Rulfo's published remarks to interviewers have reinforced this view.[9] When it is pointed out that the speech patterns and narrative forms of Jaliscan countryfolk actually recorded by ethnographers do not sound particularly like a passage out of *El llano en llamas* or *Pedro Páramo*,[10] this simplistic claim is emended, attributing to Rulfo the less painstaking but even grander virtue of having distilled the cultural essence of Jalisco and rural Mexico itself. Common to both versions of Rulfo's cultural authenticity is the notion that he has penetrated the cultural armor of the hinterland and gained access to the intimate, imaginative sources of its popular traditions. Thus, in the words of Luis Harss, Rulfo "writes about what he knows and feels, with the simple passion of a man of the land in immediate and profound contact with the elemental."[11]

II. Magical Realism Revised: From Transubstantiation to Transculturation

Probably the most systematic and critical elaboration of this thesis, with respect to both Rulfo and modern Latin-American narrative generally, is to be found in the late Angel Rama's *Transculturación narrativa en América Latina* (1982). In this work—surely one of the most significant and accomplished studies of modern Latin-American literature to have appeared in the last decade—Rama adapts the Cuban anthropologist Fernando Ortiz's conceptualization of local Latin-American culture as a "transculturation" or *neoculturación* of metropolitan models to the task of generalizing the literary phenomenon of neoregionalism, represented by authors such as Rulfo, Arguedas, Guimarães Rosa, and García Márquez. That is, unlike Carpentier, Blanco Aguinaga, Harss, and others, Rama makes explicit the anthropological premises implied in a popular cultural modernism. The neoregionalist writer, best epitomized in the figure of Arguedas, is openly characterized by Rama as a kind of partisan anthropologist, actively committed to the defense of the regional subculture, for which, at the same time, he represents the rationalizing pressures of modernization. Against the romanticized, ultimately falsifying portrayal of the neoregionalist narrator as a vatic vox populi, Rama stipulates the strictly *mediational* nature of this practice.

But what distinguishes this new, "transculturalizing" regionalism from previous models of cultural mediation via literary narrative? What makes a *Ríos profundos*, a *Grande sertão: Veredas*, or a *Pedro Páramo* qualitatively different as a discourse of mediation from a *La charca*, a *Los de abajo*, a *Doña Bárbara*, or a *La vorágine*? In attempting to answer this question, Rama once again appears to go beyond the basically impressionistic stance of Carpentier, Blanco Aguinaga, and company, whereby the alleged authenticity of the new regionalism is reduced to the workings of a romantic myth of popular communion. "The literary discourse of the regionalist novel," writes Rama.

> basically responded to the cognitive structures of the European
> bourgeoisie. This being so, it operated at the same distance, in relation
> to the content it was elaborating, as that which separated the educated
> language of the narrator from the popular language of the characters.
> This linguistic discordance replicated the discordance between content
> and discursive structure.[12]

That is, the older regionalism maintained, in accordance with its positivist ideological assumptions, a fundamental cognitive distance between its own discursive locus—that of Reason and Civilization—and that of its objective content or *materia*, preconceived as a site deprived of rational discourse. This "distance" manifests itself in the structure of the literary text itself as the gap separating the "educated" speech of the authorial voice (sometimes dramatically represented in a principal character—for example, *Dona Bárbara*'s Santos Luzardo) from the regional dialect spoken by the local characters. A break occurs, however, leading to a supersedence of the underlying positivist episteme and its logic of Otherness. Rama attributes this break—or "bracketing," as he more carefully describes it—to the agency of the avant-garde (*T*, p. 48; my translation).

Rama's vagueness about the material-historical forces that might enable the vanguard departure itself represents a crucial weak spot in the argument, and one that might seem to justify its dismissal as, in the end, simply a reversion to the mythic account of aesthetic agency that Rama had seemed, on some level, committed to overcoming. For the moment, however, I will merely note the developments that issue from this ruptural moment according to the literary-historical trajectory Rama constructs. These are: "the social novel," which preserves the positivist episteme while reversing its evaluative hierarchies (as in Vallejo's *Tungsteno*); the "critical-realist novel," which adapts the aesthetic "revolution" of the avant-garde to certain socially realistic ends (the novels of Carpentier, for example); the most characteristically vanguard current, denoted by Rama as "cosmopolitan narrative," and whose major exponent is, of course, Borges; and, finally, the neoregionalist, transcultural tendency—the highest stage, as it now becomes apparent, of the postpositivist modern dialectic per se. The final piece of the model now falls neatly into place: with the collapse of the wall separating the discursive *ratio* from its narrated object, the radically alienating effect of all previous mediations disappears. The way is now clear for the neoregionalist to enter into a properly transcultural, synthesizing compact with the indigenous or local cultural base. "The rupture of this logical system frees up the real substance belonging to the internal cultures of Latin America and makes it possible to appreciate them in other dimensions" (*T*, p. 53; my translation). This compact remains mediational in nature, but its poles are reversed, in that the *ratio* now operates in defense of, rather than against, the cultural subjects who form its specific object of representation.

The concrete, textual signal that this union has been achieved can take various specific forms, all of which, however, reduce to one essential transformation—the erasure of the characteristic linguistic hierarchy separating educated speech, *lengua culta*, from *lengua popular*. Rama bears quoting at length here:

> The author has become reintegrated with the linguistic community and speaks from within it, with unimpeded use of its idiomatic resources. If that community is, as often occurs, of rural type, or borders on an indigenous speech group, then it is starting from this linguistic system that the writer works, no longer attempting to imitate a regional speech from without but, rather, to elaborate it from within, with an artistic goal. From the moment that he no longer perceives himself outside it, and instead recognizes the linguistic community without embarrassment or belittlement as his own, he abandons the copying . . . of its irregularities and variations with respect to an academic norm and, in turn, investigates the possibilities that it provides him for the construction of a specific literary language within its framework. Here we have the phenomenon of "neoculturation," to use Ortiz's term. If the principals of textual unification and the construction of a literary

language of exclusively aesthetic invention can be seen as corresponding
to the rationalizing spirit of modernity, by compensation the linguistic
perspective that takes up this principle restores a regional world view
and prolongs its validity in a form yet richer and more interiorized than
before. It thus expands the original world view in a way that is better
adapted, authentic, artistically solvent, and, in fact, modernized—but
without destruction of identity. (*T*, pp. 42–43; my translation)

What is clearly the advantage of the concept of mediation implicit in the phenomenon of transculturation is that it avoids the dualism that invariably results
from a static "organic" notion of culture. According to such organicism, a work
is either culturally autochthonous—in which case it directly expresses the subjective immediacy of the local culture itself—or it is irredeemably alien, an exogenous artifact with no claim to authenticity. It seems clear that no work of modern narrative prose produced in the culturally heterogeneous space of Latin
America could possibly be described in terms of such an opposition—and yet
these are the terms to which the early, left-oriented readings of Rulfo ultimately
reduced themselves. If nothing else, Rama's understanding of narrative discourse
as itself a culturally synthetic, as against a purely expressive, operation super-
sedes this critical weakness.

III. Rulfo and Transculturation: Whose Voice Are We Hearing?

But granting that the cultural politics of texts such as *El llano en llamas* and *Pedro Páramo* cannot even begin to be properly assessed except on the premise of
their mediational quality as works simultaneously in the mainstream of modernism and on its regional margins, does it thereby follow that, in works such as
these, a decisive *break* with the older, naturalizing regionalism and its positivist
episteme has occurred? Does the erasure of the traditional frontier separating the
"civilized" and "reasoned" voice of the narration per se and the "unenlight-
ened" speech of the hinterland in itself constitute a penetration of the regional
"linguistic community"? If the old, colonizing *ratio* has been silenced, is the
voice we are hearing truly that of the colonized?

Consider the example of "La Cuesta de las Comadres" from *El llano en
llamas*.[13] In this story, a narrative voice that we immediately identify as "regional" through its use of colloquial dialect spins out a remembrance of what at
first appear to be two unrelated series of events: the sudden and unexplained de-
population of the small community of *ranchos* named in the title, and the equally
suspicious activities of Remigio and Odilón Torrico, the two local *caciques* who
have remained behind. The narrator, an old *campesino* who professes his friend-
ship toward the Torrico brothers, gradually and obliquely reveals the underlying
link that solves the mystery: having lost formal ownership of the surrounding

farmland *cuando el reparto* (a reference to postrevolutionary land reforms), the Torricos exploit their title to the village plot itself, forcing the newly propertied residents to submit to extortion or abandon the settlement. All save the narrator choose the latter, leaving the strong men to fend for themselves through *bando-lerismo*. It is the recurrent Rulfian story of *deshabitación* and postrevolutionary irony.

Having brought the narrative to this point of resolution, however, the narrator makes an abrupt admission: "I killed Remigio Torrico."[14] The narrator then pro-ceeds to tell how he was confronted by his victim and accused of murdering Odilón Torrico, a charge he at first does not bother to deny. Only after he has preemptively killed his accuser with a large mending needle does he patiently explain to him his innocence: Odilón was in fact murdered in a drunken brawl with his enemies in Zapotlán. Remigio's slow and excruciating death is described in a horrendously detailed and matter-of-fact sequence, and the narrative ends as the old man recalls washing the blood out of the homespun sack he used to cart Remigio's corpse off to a ravine. The final set of images is one of Rulfo's most memorable:

> Me acuerdo que eso pasó allá por octubre, a la altura de las fiestas de Zapotlán. Y digo que me acuerdo que fue por esos días porque en Zapotlán estaban quemando cohetes, mientras que por el rumbo donde tiré a Remigio se levantaban una gran parvada de zopilotes a cada tronido que daban los cohetes.
> De eso me acuerdo.

> [I remember that it happened about in October, during the fiesta in Zapotlán. And I say I remember it was during those days because in Zapotlán they were firing rockets, and every time a rocket went off in the direction where I dumped Remigio a great flock of buzzards rose up.
> That's what I remember.][15]

For a reader attuned to the narrative signposts and motivations of a conven-tional prose realism, the initial effect produced by "La Cuesta de las Comadres" is one of perplexity and shock. A clever trap has been laid, whereby the reader, coaxed into a sympathetic and patronizing alliance with the evidently innocuous and marginal voice of the narrator, is unable to withdraw from this pact as it be-comes an intimate phenomenological account of Remigio's murder. The reader is caught by his own touristic pleasure and forced, without recourse to the media-tional buffers of morality or psychopathology, to relive an act that transgresses and throws into question the pastoral hierarchies of his initial aesthetic interest. Pleasure is thus revealed as latently prurient and morbid.

This effect, understood in the more elevated and general terms of transcultu-ration, suggests an *interiority* of discourse, a writing that appears to efface itself as an outside, authorial presence amid the spontaneous emanation of oral narrative. The shock effect produced by a narrative like "La Cuesta de las Comadres"—not shock at violence per se but at its uncodedness within the cultural whole—would, in these terms, be merely the exaggerated signal of orality, the most blatant index of a final break with what Bakhtin has called the "ultimate semantic authority" of a discourse that writes its object from without.[16] The reader, thinking himself to have been presented with what is simply an extended, monologic stretch of reported speech embedded in some rationalizing narrative frame is left with nothing to stand on.

But suppose we reread "La Cuesta de las Comadres" forewarned and conscious of its ruse. This turns out to be a quite difficult task—a fact that attests to the aesthetic powers of these narratives. Rulfo seems to strike a near-perfect synthetic balance between the effusion of speech and an opposing tendency to restrict it through lacunae and patches of silence—like the one preceding "I killed Remigio Torrico"—such that the self-consciousness of the oral narration is continually receding before the brilliant and exotic surface of what it has to tell. What such a second reading may suggest, however, even if only negatively, is that this sense of an interior plenitude of spoken cultural substance is not self-sustaining but rather the effect of the *absence* of any obvious rationalizing authority on the level of the narrative discourse as a whole. Is not this plenitude, this apparent interiority, simply the result of disappointing an expectation of "direct authorial word"?[17] Reading "La Cuesta de las Comadres," we are reminded of the way in which the aesthetic or ritual objects of a traditional, precapitalist culture are displayed in a modern museum. For all their supposed autonomy, the experience we have of such objects—if we discount the sheer sensory registration of their existence—turns out in the end to be little but the experience of being in a museum, in a space that has been set aside as a fictitious site of precapitalist communion. The particular ideology of the museum experience is to invert this order of determination, to attribute the negative enclosure of the museum space to a positive and "magical" property of the pieces themselves.

Reading Rulfo as transculturation likewise inverts and ideologizes the relation of oral to literary narrative. It proposes as a return of writing to its oral, cultural roots what may just as well be understood as its inversion—the return that marks the final phase of domination and expropriation. It is revealing, in this respect, to consider the features of a narrative form neglected by Rulfo's left cultural celebrants: the traditional Mexican folk ballad, or *corrido*. The corrido, as noted by one of its major compilers,[18] has its origins in the centuries-old, residually oral tradition of the Iberian *romance*; however, it flourished only in the relatively brief period of 1850–1930, particularly in the years of the revolution, when the *corrido* became an important popular medium of transmitting the outstanding social, political, and military deeds and events. Although typically recited or sung to assembled crowds at markets and fairs, *corridos* were also printed as handbills and sold at low cost to buyers, who would then use the written texts as the basis for further oral transmission. If the composer of the *corrido* was not an actual witness to the events portrayed, it was common practice to obtain the necessary details from newspaper accounts. "There was," writes Vicente Mendoza,

> not a single event of outstanding importance to the people itself that failed to be narrated, described, commented upon, intoned in verse, and listened to with rapt attention in the public squares—it [the *corrido*] being in truth the popular press, neither daily, nor periodical, but occasional, following the course and development of Mexican life.
> (p. vii; my translation)

Do we not have in this recuperation of a written, print culture by the still residually oral culture of the Mexican masses an especially concrete process of transculturation? And yet, both from the standpoint of narrative and artistic form, the *corrido* is the very antithesis of Rulfian writing. Compare, for example, the "Corrido de Guadalupe Pantoja," which relates, like "La Cuesta de las Comadres," the death of a predatory and unpopular outlaw:

> Salió gente de Pantoja
> tapándoles la salida
> —Aquí nos dan el dinero
> o les quitamos la vida. . . .
> Llegaron hasta la loma
> pero no encontraron nada;
> se acercaron hasta un bosque
> a esperar la madrugada.
> Señores, toda la noche
> la pasamos de velada,
> esperamos a que llegue
> esa gavilla malvada.

> [Out came Pantoja's people
> blocking their exit;
> —Here you'll give us the money
> or we'll take away your lives.
> They made it to the hill
> but didn't find anything;
> they went up next to the woods
> to wait for sunrise.
> —Your Honors, all night long
> we stayed wide awake,
> awaiting the arrival

of that wicked gang.]

(p. 157; my translation)

Here, the numerous instances of reported speech at no point take on a "heightened" or opaque quality distinct from the uniform code of representation posited in relation to both *corridista* and audience. Those whose speech is reported—the "gente de Pantoja," the mule drivers, the local magistrate, Federico the clerk, resident *rancheros*, the *corridista* as direct participant, and even Pantoja himself—have, in principle, the same access to real events as does the narrator and are not to be understood as conventional characters within a representationally recreated time-space so much as the necessary testimonial links within a structure of experience common to all. This is "speech" as it presents itself to an already speaking subject: what is *said* ("lo que dicen los díceres"), not what is spoken. That which links this instance of *decir* to an actual speech act is, in complete contrast to the Rulfian practice of creating the realistic effect of regional speech, precisely the heightened artificiality of its metrical organization. Such organization obeys, needless to say, a mnemonic logic—but a logic bounded, in turn, by the necessity of appropriating a collective knowledge that consists not in knowing the "facts" of history but in knowing what to say in order to convey what is already committed to social memory. In its disregard for the re-creation of regional, dialectal effects and its preference for narrative content, "El corrido de Guadalupe Pantoja" simply confirms that residually oral culture does not think of itself here as intrinsically opposed to writing,[19] since practically any written narrative can be reduced to its testimonial elements and committed to *corrido* form.

The point at which writing resists this appropriative chemistry is the point at which the reader is no longer a potential witness to what is read—the point, mapped by Benjamin in "The Storyteller," at which information becomes a value in itself, apart from any collective bond of memory.[20] Having passed this point, the apparently seamless shifts in narrative and discursive level that give the *corrido* its characteristic quality lose their horizontal uniformity. The flatness of the *corrido* text has collapsed into the sheer verticality of Rulfian representation, where *to read* the speech of the witness is necessarily to distinguish the outwardly estranged surface of a pure utterance that has traded its mnemonic utility for the aesthetic reflexivity of the museum exhibit.

The erasure of "direct authorial word" from the horizontal axis of the narrative, which a transcultural reading interprets as a sure sign of an epistemic break, appears, more accurately in this contrastive light, to be the result of its transfer, or displacement, to a paradigmatic position from which it is able to govern the flow of narrative as if through filtration. The semic material upon which this vertical writing operates is not composed of words or meanings in the standard morphological sense but of whole narrative utterances, macroscopic blocks of a store of oral narrative, which the invisible authorial writing selects and arranges in a predetermined syntax. In Rulfo, narrative composition seems no longer to be an instance of what the Russian formalists termed *skaz* ("a manner of narration which draws attention to itself, creating the illusion of actual oral narration")[21] but rather a manipulation practiced upon what is already *skaz*, in the manner of montage. The operating space of authorship recedes from its autonomous lodging on the level of the *énoncé*, but only in order to gain a position from which it can exercise an increased power of ideological resolution. To read in this supremely rationalizing maneuver an emancipatory release of *lengua popular* is to mistake the effect for its cause, to read as an autonomous presence what is at base simply the absence of a particular manifestation of authority. But there are no ideological vacuums. That which does *not* intervene along the horizontal axis of the narrative, that which refrains from overt explanation and rationalization in an imagined preference for the sheer difference and prerationality of what is portrayed — has not this "direct authorial word" simply "retreated" to that strategically superior position from which it is able to determine the horizontal configuration of the text as a whole? In ceasing to be the Reason that is written, that configures itself as a definite subjectified presence alongside that of the characters themselves, does not Reason become the Reason that writes, that posits itself at the outset as the negative enclosure within which a particular narrative content is to take shape? In ceasing to be read, has not the presence of an alien, externalized *lengua culta* simply confirmed that it no longer requires a recognizably narrative configuration in order to operate as ideology? Has it not become implicit in the reading itself? The transparency of writing to its regional object, understood transculturally as a failure or at least deferral of the bourgeois episteme, perhaps tells us something we are loath to hear — that this same "cognitive structure" has now learned to represent itself exclusively in the cultural/aesthetic signs of its Other. The allegories of an embattled *civilización*, which have already begun their long odyssey through Latin-American fiction with the tragic sentimentalities of Echeverría's and Mármol's *unitarios*, become superfluous in the precise degree that their real counterparts no longer require them. In their place stands an abstract, institutionalized Reason without the need for a narrative form but under continual pressure to assert authority over new and explosive counterrationalities that threaten to undermine it. What better strategy than to drape itself in the legitimate prerationality of "culture"?

IV. Modernism and Populism: Hegemonizing *Barbarie*

But it would be ingenuous to continue to project this line of interpretation in a purely hypothetical mode. What I am attempting to adduce here, as should be clear to students of modern Latin-American societies, is the logic not merely of an aesthetic rationalization but of a concrete political configuration, standardly referred to as populism. I shall assume here an at least rudimentary acquaintance with the various theories and debates over populism in Latin America.[22] For my purposes, the problem of populism may be sketched in the broader lines of Gramscian sociology as one of attaining a state of modern capitalist hegemony in a setting of political "irrationality," that is, in the absence (from the point of view of capital) of rational forms of nonstate behavior. The project of populism is thus to be likened to the project of what Gramsci designates as "civil society"[23] but here under a set of historical conditions that tend to retard and obstruct the evolution of civil society in its "classic" European form. These are the conditions of "underdevelopment": the existence in society (in less developmentalist terms) of social subjects constituted outside, and often in direct antagonism to, the mediational circuits of the modern capitalist state power. Given the historical difficulties encountered in directly penetrating and supplanting these regional and "barbaric" circuitries—those of the peasant community, the Church, *caciquismo*, and the not-infrequent movement of armed political insurgency—the consensual stability of civil society must be sought through the direct control of these nonstate circuitries themselves rather than through the traditional atomizing approach of the liberal metropolitan states (constitution of the modern "citizen"). The state must, from the literary standpoint, seek to posit itself directly within the discourse of the nonstate.

Is Rulfian narrative such a discourse of the state as nonstate? Perhaps not in any directly political sense; the aesthetic complexities of these narratives cannot be simply reduced to a "populist" program. However, the interpretive fallacies that arise in the effort to theorize these narratives as instances of transcultural synthesis may *themselves* be the result of failing to observe the poltical value of the transcultural as the ideology of that very oppressive Reason it supposedly has transcended. Already evident in Blanco Aguinaga's effort to redeem Rulfian subjectivism, the assumption that a transcultural immersion in the submodern world of regionality constitutes a real break with the colonizing, imperializing past is tantamount to the assumption that the colonizing, imperializing power itself does not undergo a similar "subjectivization"—that the power that represented itself as *civilización* is now somehow less intelligent than its cultural and artistic critics. Does not the historical experience of populist strategies of revolutionary sloganizing coupled with counterrevolutionary policy (in Mexico particularly) show the falsity of such thinking? However remote Rulfo's fiction may intrinscially be from such ploys, its evident capacity to suggest to critics and readers a "popular" aesthetic, despite the at best equivocal nature of its links to popular life, indicates a possible affinity between the aesthetics of vertical writing and the politics of the state as nonstate. Perhaps the peculiar effect whereby a rationalizing, discursive exterior disappears in the transcultural reading of Rulfo tells us that this exterior is coterminous with the ideological horizon of what is in fact not a cultural but (to invoke Gramsci once more) a *hegemonic* discourse of modernity.

To move in the direction of a reading of Rulfo that reflects this broader hegemonic optic, we must invert the logic of the transcultural model. Where readers like Blanco and Rama propose to find a liberational release of linguistic subjectivity in *El llano en llamas* and *Pedro Páramo*, we might look, on the contrary, for the signs of a palpable containment and editing of a *counterrationality* whose fully integral presence is suppressed in the narrative economy of the Rulfian text.

To see how this works, let us go back to "La Cuesta de las Comadres" and the question of its "orality." Read in its positivity as sheer, unfettered *skaz*, the story seems to float in its own cultural innocence and autonomy. A certain discrete pleasure is aroused in the reader as he supposes that he has circumvented the blockades of a naturalizing stereotypology and penetrated the authentic, subjective truth of rural Mexican folk. The shock of violence and the heightened description of the surrounding space (recall the final image of the vultures and the exploding fireworks) add the feel of sheer phenomenological presence, a physical immediacy freed of literary buffers.

Such an effect can be obtained, however, only at the cost of naturalizing the implicit, if displaced, historical and social subtext of the narrative. This is the absence of an overriding and depersonalized political and moral authority—the absence, in so many words, of a state. The murder of the Torrico brothers is forced on the local residents because of this institutional vacuum. The narrator's oral version of events in "La Cuesta de las Comadres" is delivered in lieu of an official, written deposition; his "confession" appears to conceal nothing, however, and is free of legitimizing motives. The occasion for a "cultural" experience of the events described may thus be argued to be a simple consequence of this preliminary evacuation of modern political "rationality." It is as if a still-predominant naturalist master narrative had simply deferred ideological encodement, preferring the sheer difference of *barbarie* to its rational antinomy.

The aura of "culture" that emerges from this vacuum has in its turn, however, its own repressive logic. Culture in itself becomes the naturalizing and dehistoricizing containment of what is otherwise potentially an emergence of a particular counterrationality directly opposed to that of the absent state mediation. The act recorded in "La Cuesta de las Comadres," disregarding its personalized and "regional" flavor, is, after all, the exercise of a certain political agency: the direct action of a peasant community against a violator of its law. The "oral" quality of the narrative need not, moreover, limit itself to the signifying of a "cultural" difference—orality in a more radical sense implies a meaning that is not the property of an individual subject at all but of a given collectivity or communal existence (Marx's *Gemeinwesen*). It is, in short, a signifying practice linked to a generally communal, precapitalist mode of life. The narrator's admission—"I killed Remigio Torrico"—would thus not require rationalization as an exotic, prerational affirmation of cultural innocence; rather, it would obviate such a rationalization for the very fact that it does not constitute the speaking subject as a transgressor, does not tie the speaker to a code of behavior in which his "crime" can be determined and assessed. Oral narrative in its broad social and historical setting implies an intersubjectivity[24] unfamiliar to written/state institutions of nationality and jurisprudence. The narrator would thus not be personally implicated in the deaths of the Torricos at all. Instead, his discourse would be prompted by a much more basic motive, which is that of conveying an "experience" (*Erfahrung*), in Benjamin's sense.[25] His actions would be meaningless outside the larger experience of *deshabitación* and the measures taken to reverse this process through combatting directly the practice of *bandolerismo*.[26] In killing Remigio, the narrator would simply be affirming the right of the community to render judgment and carry out sentence on those who violate its constitution.

This is, of course, not the narrative we read in "La Cuesta de las Comadres" but rather the one we are, as it were, preempted from reading in exchange for the offer of its "cultural" and fetishized image. It is, as a general rule, the same economy that operates throughout Rulfo's fictions: the interest and pleasure of the reader is everywhere caught by the screen image of a brilliant, folkloric microcosm in which the state, the historical rationality of modern capitalist society, is necessarily deferred as a narrative figure, always held in abeyance, but never, as a result, made to appear in its full social and historical contingency. The state thus tends to be preconsciously situated as an innocent backdrop to culture, an invisible surface upon which are projected the images of a life that is quintessentially "Mexican" but without political or historical mediation.

What enables this two-dimensional rendering of a state that was previously a fully rounded, if coded, narrative presence? And is this new rendering really the decisive rupture with naturalism that the transcultural reading of Rulfo presupposes it to be? Here I could only respond with the sketchings of a theory requiring a broader and more investigative study than can presently be undertaken. Of central importance is the historical conjuncture in which Rulfian narrative is both produced and disseminated, not merely in terms of the well-known postpopulist and counterrevolutionary shifts in social and cultural policy with the onset of *alemanismo* and their effect on Rulfo but in the broader terms of the changed relationship between Mexican intellectuals generally and a new, institutionalized phase of hegemonic consolidation. The word I would tentatively use to characterize this new relationship is "demobilization": the intellectual type that "comes of age" in the 1950s (best eptimoized, no doubt, in the figure of Octavio Paz and in the "Mexican" philosophy of *El laberinto de la soledad*) encounters for perhaps the first time since the revolution a kind of cultural buffer zone in which the immediate demands of partisanship and class conflict appear to have been suspended. In point of fact, the state itself has generated its own corps of "organic intellectuals" in a highly rationalized system of bureaucracy; it no longer has a direct need for intellectual-revolutionary titans of the Vasconcelos type, since the latter have effectively deposited their own cybernetic animus in an operating cultural officialdom. The state has in this special sense erased itself by assuming shape as the abstract, institutional horizon within which a wayward literary talent is "free" to develop and "experiment" with representationalities heretofore dictated by the immediacies of a still-unsettled phase in the consolidation of hegemonic power. Realism can now take on the appearance of a mere aesthetic convention, reality itself having been cemented in place by a successful and self-reproducing hegemony. It is this demobilized intellect, with all that its existence presupposes, that as a moment in a certain sociological dialectic coincides with the literary-aesthetic moment of . . . modernism.

Rulfian narrative's particular activation and reconfiguration of what are, a priori, the ideological and representational parameters of the modernist conjuncture in Mexico suggests, in its turn, a severe perplexity and estrangement from the revolutionary process that has made the modern Mexican state into a reality. *Pedro Páramo* and *El llano en llamas* give us the revolutionary period "made strange," but only as a middle-class intellect—itself the offspring of the revolution, even if it no longer needs to dwell on its origins—could estrange it. A "populist" image of the masses must still be rendered, for the reason that this representational vessel has become the bearer of a hegemonic discourse of postrevolutionary national identity. But any historical consciousness of the populist subtext has fallen away, having been effectively obviated by the success of an abstracted and historically "autonomous" state power in steering mass antagonisms into manageable conduits of institutional mediation. Into this breach there has resurfaced that essentially pathological code of representation that had never been fully eradicated from the discourse of the "revolutionary" novel itself. The mass or "regional" subject is accordingly "understood" as the site of spontaneous and instinctive propensities for violent and "irrational" behavior, the results of a diseased social organism. Sadism, vendetta, parricide, incest, and religious hysteria—these are the traditional motifs of a literary current that includes not only the notorious narrative tracts of creole racism (Zeno Gandías's *La charca*, for example, or Cambaceres's *En la sangre*) but also, if more ambiguously, the "revolutionary" narratives of an Azuela, a Yáñez, even a Revueltas. Here I am only following Rama's mapping of naturalism. But are these not the same ideological clots around which form the characters of Rulfian narrative? Is there not expressed, throughout the entire "inframundane" world of Rulfian fiction, a profound continuity with the hoary vision of *barbarie* evoked in Sarmiento—even if defamiliarized and displaced by the self-conscious representationalities of modernism?

Against its naturalist or at least premodern forebears, Rulfian transcultural narrative is read as emanating from within a speech-totality (*comunidad lingüística*) that had heretofore made its appearance in fictional prose strictly as exteriorized displays of reported speech. I have already indicated the aesthetic fallacies of this particular reading, attempting to show that the specific locus of authority and writing in Rulfo has not merged into the cultural base but, rather, shifted into a vertical position from which it becomes simultaneous and coterminous with narrative economy as such. I have further proposed that the "authorial word" in Rulfo loses its horizontal configuration and becomes transparent to a culturally (or transculturally) oriented criticism, not as a result of any purely aesthetic or "epistemic" rupture (as both orthodox modernism and Rama's Foucauldian schematic claim) but because the state, the very center of extraliterary authority, has itself become a horizon of representation, invisible except in the negative image of its Other.

Transcultural theory understands this as the mediational relation it is but gives it an affirmative cultural interpretation. However, is it not culture itself that is thereby made to assume the rationalizing function of *civilización* by suspending the real, historical contradictions of the social process? And is it not this aura of cultural transcendence that marks the departure of Rulfian narrative from a tradition of pathologizing naturalism with which it is otherwise entirely continuous? So long as this cultural optic is in place, the conflicting claims of modernism and realism can themselves be kept in suspension, allowing a transculturalized Rulfo to evade what might otherwise be a line of criticism concerned with the evident estrangement of Rulfian narrative from a *historical* subject whose portrayal—if I may be so unrepentantly Lukácisian as to say so—is fundamentally what matters in the break with naturalism and positivism. In attempting to clarify its connections with the discursive configurations of populism, I have already suggested that Rulfian fiction represents a step back, or aesthetic remove, from the direct appeal to "the people" that we expect to find in "revolutionary" populist literature. Perhaps it would be more accurate to say that in transculturalizing the ethical and "scientific" perplexities of a middle class engulfed in a revolutionary upheaval that threatens to exceed its own interests, Rulfian narrative is really a culmination of the populist tradition, its adaptation to relations of force and an ideological configuration in which the masses can neither be rationalized away nor denied a narrative presence. The consciousness of a "cultural" identity in which all "Mexicans" share the same quasi-genetic national traits offers a certain rationalization of the "irrational" under conditions of postpopulist stalemate. If it is Paz who gives this conjuncture its classic philosophical expression, it is Rulfo who endows it with all the imaginative authenticity of a popular-cultural unconscious. The dormant but potentially volcanic violence of an incessant class struggle is ideologically managed and contained on the level of its "cultural" experience. "Culture" in this sense has no material or historical reference. It becomes a mere postulate, a strictly mediatory concept, made necessary by the incompatibility of two representationalities—the one in which "the people" are invoked as the subject of official revolutionary History; and the other, less apparent but more entrenched and virulent, in which the specter of *barbarie* is repeatedly conjured by a pathological hatred and fear of the masses.

V. Talking Alterity: *The Cotton Pickers*

How then are we to evaluate the cultural politics of Rulfian narrative? Which, if any, of the antagonistic historical and social projects in Mexico and the world is furthered or accommodated by this literature? There seems little doubt that, when held up to the worst extremes of avant-garde hermeticism and naturalist pathologizing realism, transcultural narrative appears to have made substantial advances. The discourse of the cultural seems intuitively preferable, for all its ideology, to those of aesthetic theology or biological determinism. But to what do we attribute these advances, and at what point must we conclude that what seem to be the literary or representational embodiments of social advance have, in reality, become strategies for its containment?

This much, I think, can be stated without equivocation: Rulfo's transcultural modernization of Mexican and Latin-American traditions of narrative is progressive to the precise degree to which the broader hegemonic transformation that endows Rulfian narrative with its particular "subject effect" can be characterized as progressive. We are, that is, once again confronted with the question of the state. The principle defect of the redemptive line of interpretation of Rulfo and transcultural narrative followed by Rama, Blanco Aguinaga, and others is its failure to consider whether the affirmation of the "regional" has not already become the ideology of a revised and culturally intelligent form of imperialist hegemony. Of course, to pose such a question is not to answer it; a real labor of investigation and critique is required to produce an answer that may itself vary over the historical and spatial expanse we perhaps overgeneralize with the term "Latin America." But failing to pose this question—which is also the question of nationalism—the result can only be ideology in place of criticism.

I do not claim here to have carried out all the analytical and critical steps required to render political verdicts on the writing of Juan Rulfo. It seems clear, given the present crisis in Mexican society, that such verdicts are still waiting for the historical outcome that will permit them to assume more than a purely academic significance. I can, however, suggest a means of framing the question of value as it is raised by the Rulfian texts. The strategy here is Benjamin's: to contrast the various narrative possibilities worked out in Rulfo not to the Tradition against which the modernity of Rulfo is affirmed but to other possible and historically existing narratives that "break" with tradition at a different point and with, perhaps, an alternative historical trajectory.

The alternative work I have in mind here is a novel written under the notorious pseudonym B. Traven. First published in German under the title *Der Wobbly* (1928), its English translation appeared as *The Cotton Pickers* in 1956.[27] Through its first-person narrator, Gales, the novel relates the life of an international assortment of itinerant laborers in northeastern Mexico during the Obregón presidency. Its connections to Rulfo's later novels are vague and seemingly arbitrary, since few conventional marks of literary influence or genetic affinity are evident. B. Traven (thought now by some to be the German radical writer Ret Marut) is a resident alien in Mexico and started writing at least a generation earlier than Rulfo, in a narrative tradition difficult to identify (the proletarian novel?) but clearly marginal to the genealogical line that Rulfo inherited (and projected).

Carefully read, *The Cotton Pickers* exposes the cultural politics of Rulfo by short-circuiting the evaluative criteria of the transcultural model itself. Like Rulfo and transcultural narrative, *The Cotton Pickers* can be read as participating in a movement to transform a classical master narrative of European realism by rewriting it through the direct experience of a social subject excluded from modern metropolitan representationalities. In contrast to the regional or "oral" cultural realism of Rulfo, however, Traven's narrative never permits the cultural to fix itself as a self-identical object of representation. Instead of a brilliantly contrived and exotic oral-cultural screen upon which, in narrative scenes, are projected all the various perplexities of a modern bourgeois subject in an "underdeveloped" setting, *The Cotton Pickers* presents us with, to all appearances, the utterly familiar and universal parable of *labor*—looking for it, finding it, and surviving it. Labor, without ever reaching the level of its concept, without ever being named except in its immediate forms as cotton picking, baking, cattle herding, and so on, becomes the propelling force of a narrative that effectively suspends the representationality of national, cultural, or regional difference. At the same time that these orders of difference, which mark the point of departure of the transcultural, are displaced, however, the representational space in which their sameness is affirmed is withheld. The result is that the dialectic of the Other takes on an ironic, comic aspect, as if it were the butt of a tacit joke. The first section of the novel particularly exemplifies this quality: Gales, the gringo narrator, finds himself on an isolated railroad platform on his way to a cotton plantation of uncertain location. Here he meets Charley, "the gigantic Negro"; Abraham, "the little Negro from New Orleans"; Sam Woe, "the Chink"; Antonio, the mestizo; and Gonzalo, the Indian—all bound for the same cotton field, all in the same predicament. With the exception of Gonzalo and Antonio, none of them can pronounce the long Nahual name of the place the labor contractors have told them to find. Initially mistrustful of one another, they group together and head off into the bush in search of their common destination. Having all emerged from a seemingly spontaneous code of racial or ethnic types, however, the characters immediately begin to behave in ways that cast into disuse the order of difference they invoke, since nothing in what they do or in what happens to them suggests or requires ethno-pathological explanation. It is as if labor were visible to itself only through the eyes of labor, capital having been ousted from its various insinuated forms of "popular" subjectivity.

Do we not observe here the configurations of a subject that is, so to speak, both previous to and beyond the transcultural, a subject that is never permitted to emerge in the "magical" apparitions and vanishings of Rulfian fiction? To take this contrast even further, we can observe that in Traven, too, writing loses its rationalizing profile, not by rendering the negative space of an exhibited orality but by refusing to radically differentiate itself from the reported speech of its characters. There is a *corrido*-like flatness of register in *The Cotton Pickers*, which can perhaps be explained as the effect of a gravitational force exerted on the narrative by the experience of associated wage labor as such. Speech in this world simply lacks the time or motive necessary to cultivate its own reified image as against the transparent rationality of the written. Writing and speech begin to lose their distinct outlines in a third reality of sheer *talk* as the direct testimonial link between subjects. As with pathological orders of difference, the writing/speech duality never actually evacuates the narrative, but in remaining on its horizon it nevertheless becomes inoperative and laughable. The narrator-protagonist Gales writes like the conventional first person, talking to himself "publically," but the publicity of this speech lacks any privilege as against the reported speech of others, and is, in fact, always on the point of being extended and duplicated in the speech of others. That which is given here as the continual frustration and outflanking of a representationality centered on the reified presence of the Other, seems to be simply a popular recognition that the Other has no real empirical weight, that it belongs not to the order of things but to the order of language.

Is *The Cotton Pickers* a Mexican novel? Evidently not in the same way that *Pedro Páramo* is a Mexican novel. Perhaps the best way to answer is that these are the novels of a geographically shared space in which two social and ideological projects—indeed, two histories—are situated, one overshadowed and obscured in the authoritative presence of the other. The ideological project of Rulfian narrative is to invent "Mexico," to endow with all the authority of a human and mythological nature what increasingly becomes the abstractly postulated domain of a state in the hands of capital. ("The nation," writes Robert Fossaert in *La sociétée*, "is the discourse of the state.")[28] *The Cotton Pickers*, on the other hand, is written in isolation from this anxiety, not as a novel of statelessness (for who could say what such a novel would be?) but as a novel of the between states, a narrative of the modern "transnational labor force." Perhaps I could go even further and suggest, on the supposition that Traven was a refugee from the failed German Revolution of 1919, that *The Cotton Pickers* is the narrative of a European anti-imperialism that has recognized its own impossibility except on the periphery of the History that is its initial ground—a narrative that has refused to erect itself on the ideological disappointments of "the revolution that never happened"[29] and hence a kind of antimodernism. Be this as it may, Traven's book cannot be denied its place as a lateral, "suppressed lineage" alongside Rulfo and the transcultural modernists and offers, in my view, a model of postnaturalist narrative more capable than the Rulfian of articulating, from the standpoint of its enemies, the present realities of imperialism. *The Cotton Pickers* at least begins the task of elaborating the representationalities of historical subjects that in Rulfo are always an absence—those invisible people who have left the Cuestas de las Comadres, the Luvinas, and the Comalas to Rulfo's galleries of the living dead and who now amass themselves in the great settlements of Nezahuacóyotl and in the cheap labor colonies along either side of the U.S. border.

Chapter 4
Modernism as *Cultura Brasileira:*
Eating the "Torn Halves"

1. Paz and [Ching——]: The Transcultural Signifier

Gramsci begins his *Notes on Italian History* by advancing a theory of the state as the "historical unity of the ruling classes." "But it would be wrong," he continues, "to think that this unity is simply juridical and political . . . ; the fundamental historical unity, concretely, results from the organic relations between state or political society and 'civil society.' "[1] On the Italian bourgeois revolution, Gramsci's central object of theorization in the *Notes*, it is proposed that the "historical unity" of the Italian bourgeoisie is first realized outside the juridical-political sphere through a "passive revolution," or "war of position," in which the cultural movement of *risorgimento* plays a significant, if not crucial, role. The eventual conquest and consolidation of state power becomes possible as a result of this preceding integration of the various nonstate "autonomies" of civil society into the locus of an essentially transpolitical power that goes by the theoretical name of "hegemony."

What is most immediately striking to anyone who studies the modern Latin-American social formations is the broadly consistent way in which their history calls forth the articulated concepts of the Gramscian theory of hegemony, while at the same time inverting their sequence. The crucial factor in this apparent inversion is, of course, that of colonization. That "historical unity of the ruling classes" that—whether as fait accompli or mere postulate—marks the Latin-American bourgeois revolution begins not with integration but with separation. It is only the initial class (or, perhaps, intraclass) unity, "simply juridical and political," that enables "independence," or the definitive break with the mercantile-colonial state power, to become historically realized. The fact that, in real economic and political terms, the incipiently independent national formation has only exchanged a mercantilist for a "free market" dependency, Spain for England, does not at all lessen the subsequent social and ideological impact of this inversion. The incipient Latin-American state, however primitive and politically circumscribed, becomes the condition, the sine qua non, for a bourgeois revolution that commences its nonorthodox and highly contradictory development not only in the absence of an effective base in civil society but, ideologically speaking, without a unitary bourgeois subject. The crucial objective of bourgeois revolution thus becomes not the conquest of state power in the political-juridical sense but the *conquest of civil society*. From the very first the state finds itself enmeshed in an acute crisis orginating in its own abstract negativity as an autonomous power. Although it must continually face external threats to its existence and may, within the global relations of power, represent little more than a semiautonomous commercial agency, the state undergoes its severest test in the struggle to overcome its own purely political abstraction by synthesizing the real class subject it is supposed, in a classically Marxist sense, to represent. What it lacks is precisely what the modern European nation-state, as understood by Gramsci, presupposes: hegemony.

The modern history of Latin America bears witness to the profound and still-unresolved contradictions entailed in this crisis of hegemony. In its extreme form it manifests itself as the paradoxical tendency for the state, in order to maintain the ever more narrowly constituted "historical unity" of its class basis, to actively suppress those very "autonomies" of civil society (which represent its only possibility of redemption) because they have begun to stray into the camp of opposing class interests. Such is the case of the so-called bureaucratic authoritarian regimes.[2] But even in such postrevolutionary societies as Mexico, Cuba, and Nicaragua—putting aside the question of their real and apparent political variations on the bourgeois revolutionary theme—the effects of inversion can be traced in the intense debates and struggles that surround the question of nationality itself, especially as it effects the sphere of the cultural. Although, in keeping with methodological conventions bequeathed by the history of the "classical" European states, there is a spontaneous tendency to speak of the national cultures of Cuba or Mexico as the subjects of broad intellectual consensus, the reality is that the sphere of the cultural throughout the modern Latin-American social formations remains intensely disputed. The more "modern" the state that Gramsci denotes as "political society"—the more the state throws off the traditional oligarchical and *caciquista* heraldries of its rule to assume the mantle of the abstract rationality of governmental bureaucracies—the more problematic and charged the question of the nation as a cultural entity becomes.

When Martí in "Nuestra América" accused the Latin-American governing elites of failing to base governance on an understanding of the "natural" man and ridiculed their slavish adherence to the abstract political rationalities of Europe, he perhaps lacked the concepts that would have prevented his criticism from falling back into what now appears to be an equally anachronistic position of political romanticism. This essay's strong contemporary resonance in Latin-American ideological debate, however, suggests that it was not Martí's reversion to Rousseau but his own unschooled appreciation of a dialectical reality that was already gaining the upper hand. What Martí posits but cannot conceive in his appeal for a "natural" art of governance is, precisely, hegemony: that space of real mediation in which what appear to him as two equally unacceptable alternatives—the *barbarie* of organic society and the inorganic artifice of *civilización*—negate each other in the utopia of the modern nation.

Returning again to the critique of Rulfian, transcultural narrative, we might formulate its modernizing breakthrough as the discovery, from the perspective of the above-mentioned historical inversion, of one possible formula or system of coordinates for a projected autononmous and hegemonic national space. If, (as in Fossaert's phrase),[3] the nation itself may be "read" as the preeminent discourse—the master narrative—of the state, then the task for an inverted bourgeois revolution is not simply the authoritative command over this discourse (in the sense of an uncontested right to its exercise and to the designation of its official mouthpieces) but, more crucially, the production per se of this discourse as the synthetic carrier of a national myth of identity. The state must, sooner or later, intervene directly in the real synthesis of its discursive "nation effect."

I have argued that in Rulfian narrative such intervention takes the form of a negation in which the state's traditional coded presence as a rationalizing "ultimate semantic authority" of narrative, its effective regionalization of all that does not pertain to its central, "civilizing" authority, "disappears" from the horizontal axis of discourse. Left behind is a kind of purified culture-scape, which appears, in its positivity, as autonomous and self-generating. The effectiveness of this model of autonomization lies in the fact that the heteronomizing, "rational" element has developed to the point that it can manifest itself negatively as the ground or "condition of possibility" for a narrative discourse thereby endowed with the appearance of simple cultural immanence. The state, as a principle of political domination, learns to resolve provisionally the contradiction of its negative "independence" by agreeing not to name itself, while at the same time it rigidly codifies the meaning of its as yet prehegemonized domain under the general heading of "culture." No one has to prove that the folkloric *inframundo* of *Pedro Páramo* and *El llano en llamas* exudes *mexicanidad*, despite the fact that the narratives themselves never once invoke this quality by name. This is somehow always already the obvious fact. *Civilización* advances in its contradictory campaign against *barbarie* by gradually monopolizing the rights to its signification, displacing skillfully in the process the growing sense that it is an imperialized *civilización* itself that has come to teach the authentic meaning of barbarism. The line of interpretation that comes to affirm such a nation effect as the direct expression of a preexisting authenticity and autonomy of culture not only stands the inverse structure of bourgeois revolution back, as it were, on its head. By excluding the question of hegemony, it effectively reproduces the state's very ideological drive to resolve its extraterritoriality through its "spontaneous" derivation in the organic spatial coordinates of "culture."

The real, objective limits placed on this mode of narrative prefiguration of hegemonic space may at first be difficult to perceive, since the orthodox reading process itself—as registered in the existence of a "reading formation"[4] corresponding to the literary principles of the transcultural—presupposes its functioning. The ideal subject of bourgeois hegemony and the actual reading subject *formally* coincide in the restricted sense that they simultaneously occupy the same site. But the negative transparency of *civilización*, the positioning of the estranged *ratio* outside the narrative as its discrete frame—which is what makes the superimposition possible in the first place—obtains its particular effectiveness through a rigid separation of spatial regions which the independent motion of either in the direction of the boundary that separates them continually threatens to blur. Such rigidity shows itself in Rulfian narrative not only as the liberating absence of any openly rationalizing voice or code but equally as an implicit constraint on content itself, requiring that it never exceed the range of behaviors, settings, and so on, that befit the only once-removed demands of a pathological examination. The Rulfian collective hero is never openly accused of the social irrationalities that exclude him from the mainstream of History, but at the same time he cannot cross the line that separates him from *civilización*. He cannot question the authority that exonerates him in the name of culture.

But what if the *ratio* itself attempts to reenter the space it has placed outside itself as the site of its imaginary, "cultural" mediation? To answer, we might refer to another classical text of the modern Mexican tradition, Octavio Paz's *The Labyrinth of Solitude*. In the chapter entitled "The Sons of La Malinche," Paz in fact begins by posing the very problem of separation as an apparently vitiating effect of transcultural narrative:

> The European considers Mexico to be a country on the margin of
> universal history, and everything that is distant from the center of his
> society strikes him as strange and impenetrable. The peasant—remote,
> conservative, somewhat archaic in his ways of dressing and speaking,
> fond of expressing himself in traditional modes and formulas—has
> always had a certain fascination for the urban man. In every country he
> represents the most ancient and secret element of society. For everyone
> but himself he embodies the occult, the hidden, that which surrenders
> itself only with great difficulty: a buried treasure, a seed that sprouts in

the bowels of the earth, an ancient wisdom hiding among the folds of the land.[5]

The formula, in so many words, for Rulfo. But, Paz continues,

It is noteworthy that our images of the working class are not colored with similar feelings, even though the worker also lives apart from the center of society, physically as well as otherwise, in districts and special communities. But how can we explain the fact that in the great revolutionary novels the proletariat again does not provide the heroes, merely the background? (Pp. 66–67)

How indeed? This is the question that the hasty dialectic of transcultural identity takes care to defer. Paz answers himself with a standard piece of dogma—"The modern worker lacks individuality" (p. 67)—but the really critical rejoinder echoes through clearly enough: the modern proletariat cannot be so easily mapped into the cultural coordinates of hegemonic space. In effect, the hegemonic formula embodied in Rulfo's negative regionalism is criticized not for its fetishism but for its neglect of a potential site of counterhegemonic agency that might not be so easily articulated within the organic-cultural version of *mexicanidad*. Even if it is true that the working class "lives apart from the center of society," this is not a remoteness *from* the center but a remoteness *within* the center; the figure of encirclement here ceases to be merely an ideological metaphor for what, in terms of actual hegemonic space, is the circumscribing containment of a rural, regional subject. It becomes both spatially and hegemonically literal. To repeat, Comala is not Nezahuacóyotl.

What Paz implicitly calls for here is a "de-centering" of hegemonic space— or, more precisely, its *apparent* de-centering as part of a discrete mobilization of the center itself, allowing it to break through its immediate encirclement and assume multiple but uniformly molecular shape at every given spatial coordinate. Bearing in mind the peculiar semiotic law of the Rulfian transcultural text— whereby the signified, in order to attain that level at which it is seen to identify itself freely and spontaneously as *mexicanidad* (or, in the more abstract and theoretical discourse of Rama, as "orality" or "culture"), must itself ward off every attempt of the (real or supposed) agency of signification to occupy the horizontal axis of the narrative—it now becomes possible to indicate what is forefeited by the signified in such a quid pro quo as this very same mobile and molecular autonomy. The autonomy of the signified in Rulfo is equivalent to its immobilization as signified, to the absolute prohibition on its movement back into the fluid substance of cultural signifying. I have discussed the paradoxical form assumed by this autonomy as an orality effect—the "aura," or fetish meaning, of oral tradition—which works only on the condition that orality itself surrender any claim to its own poetic principle. The flavor of orality is purchased at the price of banishing every hint of its mediational presence. The effort to reintegrate and, at the same time, de-center this rigid severance of *mexicanidad* from its day-to-day discursive existence would accordingly require the discovery of a site from which the negativity of the signified could, as it were, speak itself ''democratically.'' If the Rulfian-transcultural moment achieves the initial autonomy of *mexicanidad* from the rationalizing discourse that posits it in a gesture of colonizing contempt, the next step must be that in which the nation effect returns from its self-isolation to be reinvested with the discursivity of a postcolonial subject. Signified and signifier are to meet again on a ground that is not that of the cultural artifact but that of language itself as the very creative and fluid energy of the cultural.

Paz himself seems to project this linguistic, molecularizing formula for a hegemonic space in his now-classical reading of Mexican obscenities, specifically of the manifold signifier *chingar*.

> The word is our sign and seal. By means of it we recognize each other
> among strangers, and we use it every time the real conditions of our
> being rise to our lips. To know it, to use it, to throw it in the air like a
> toy, or to make it quiver like a sharp weapon is a way of affirming that
> we are Mexican. (p. 74)

As signifier, *chingar*—more exactly, [ching— —]—projects an integration of national, hegemonic space as an orality, but one that simultaneously transcends its own regionalized, premodern immobilization. The utterance [ching— —] is a writing, the manifestation of a creative, ratiocinative subjectivity that also speaks—not, like the transcultural text, a writing that must sacrifice its subjective character in order to generate what is merely a speech effect. [Ching— —] is equivalent to *mexicanidad* at the level of the signifier, the auto-signification of national identity.

Unfortunately for the hegemonic project articulated by Paz, however, the dialectic does not come to rest here. For despite the formal autonomy of [ching— —] as a term that means ''everything and nothing''—indeed, in contradiction of this abstract fluidity—there is a constraint placed on its meaning:

> But in this plurality of meanings the ultimate meaning always contains
> the idea of aggression, whether it is the simple act of molesting,
> pricking, or censuring, or the violent act of wounding or killing. (p. 76)

It seems that the signifier cannot escape the logic of aggressiveness (particularly masculine aggression) that initially liberates it from the bondage of the cultural signified. Ultimately, according to Paz, it taints the subject with the pathological ''servile morale,'' which, for the author, represents the tragic flaw of *mexicanidad*. ''No one uses it . . . in public'' (p. 77). That is, to the degree that it opens up a space for the synthetic presence of civil society, this space in turn is instantly occupied by the same irrational, personalist structures of social behavior that signify the continual impossibility of modern civil society. Like the "institutional Revolution" itself, [ching— —] suffers the pathological condition of corruption. Although it establishes the *formal* space of a synthetic civil society, it contradicts its own formal principle by enabling the irrational subject of *barbarie* to operate the synthesis. The *ratio*, having discovered a likely niche, is once more put to flight. One result of this is the discourse of *The Labyrinth of Solitude* itself, the discourse that cites [ching— —] but must itself refrain from its utterance. In the end Paz has been lead back to the old positivist creed of the *porfiriato*, which the revolution was assumed to have expunged. Having approached the problem of modernity with a greater sense of its hegemonic requirements, Paz can do no more than contemplate its absence from a higher, essentially ironic, and pessimistic standpoint.

What conclusions may be drawn from this apparently final concession to the stigma of the irrational? From the standpoint of the historical problematic that I have identified as the drive of an "inverted" bourgeois revolution to complete and realize itself through the integrating synthesis of a hegemonic space, all that can be said categorically is that the hegemonizing project more or less typified in the Rulfian narrative model (and in which we may include the modern transcultural classics—Arguedas, Guimarães Rosa, and so on—identified by Rama) "works" only to the degree that it reflects what is already the fait accompli of a modernization that has broken the counterhegemonic resistance of rural centers of traditional oligarchical power. This success, however, does not resolve but only heightens the contradictions inherent in the abstract autonomy of the state itself, which, even if it commands as a political power the space in which it was once opposed as a foreign presence, still struggles to find a way of populating it with the "civil" subjects who are to function as its molecular units. Paz's ironizing and cynical epitomization of this subject as the one who says [ching— —] bears witness to both the real and the hallucinatory obstacles that stand between' the "reason of state" and the territorialized reason of its would-be hegemony.

II. *Antropofagia*: Cultural Autonomy as Consumptive Production

There is a familiar line of thought at work, even if also continually resisted, in all efforts to resolve the question of how to define modernity in a peripheral setting. This line is to reject the question itself as unanswerable, since (no matter how much one qualifies it) the idea of modernity itself is a European invention—that is, an inescapably alien, extraterritorial logic that will always end up by exposing the "dependency" of any local or regional claim to have discovered its synthetic principle. In the striving to *be* modern consists the very antithesis of the modern as such. "Dependency" is accordingly understood as being more than the misfortune of neocolonial status; it is, rather, the very logic of a historical subject that never catches up, that never "makes History" except in the image of an already-made. We can find this idea variously articulated throughout the writing of Latin-American essayists in particular, from Paz to V. S. Naipaul. But even so militant and avant-garde a text as Carpentier's 1949 prologue to *El reino de este mundo* seems, in a more roundabout way, to affirm this logic, by declaring the independence of the Latin-American imagination from a standard of purely intellectual experience that, even if it is refused as decadent, does not thereby relinquish its claim to represent the latest historical trend. The conclusion suggested by this seemingly latent crisis of historical self-identity is that the *intellectual* project of modernization, regardless of the real political successes achieved, experiences itself as inherently contradictory and disappointing. The modern, even in the presence of its indices as an incremental process of social, economic, and political "modernization," withholds itself as their overall, spontaneous, and synthesizing representation.

But it would be false to generalize such melancholy, if for no other reason than because the opposite, affirmative pole of this dialectic is also detectable among the texts and traditions that make up modern Latin-American literary and cultural history. For the problem may be thought out differently: the modern depends, for a sense of its own identity, on a spatial region of the not-modern (as its "trace," to employ the jargon of deconstruction), and it is the modern's very *dependency* that now offers a locus of *autonomy* to the not-modern. The moment of the most abject dependency, by seemingly offering no resistance to the rationalizing agency of the modern, colonizing culture, derives from this extreme unevenness the strategic advantage of being able to trump the superior power. It does this by first enclosing the antagonist in its own space and then simply withholding itself.

Such, at least, is the "guerrilla" strategy for cultural autonomy drawn up by the Brazilian writer Oswald de Andrade in *Manifesto Pau-Brasil* (1924) and *Manifesto antropofago* (1928), two of the founding documents of the Brazilian avant-garde, known in Portuguese as *modernismo*. Thus in Oswald's own application of the formula for a *poesia pau-brasil*, the very texts of discovery and conquest (the *roteiros*, or ship logs of the Portuguese conquerors) are reduced to fragments and then selectively quoted in a constellation that confirms not the authority that encloses the newly discovered space and appropriates it but rather "Brasil"'s gradual seduction of the discourse of discovery itself, and the drawing out, as it were, of its own latent will to *barbarie*. As *pau-brasil*—that is, as Brazil wood, the colony's legendary first export commodity, from which the name of the national territory itself is drawn—the poetic discourse of *cultura brasileira* outflanks the Reason of *civilización*, by preempting the moment of appropriation in which the original enclosure and priority of rational discursive space is reaffirmed and restored. *Poesia pau-brasil* literally *expropriates* itself, becoming a *poesia de exportação* (poetry for export), but only at that point that will reveal the dominant cultural discourse as nothing but the repressed and sublimated drive to return to this alien substance, which turns out to have been Reason's own initial ground and point of origin. In Oswald's *pau-brasil* restructuring of the texts of discovery—unlike the transculturalizing texts of modern neoregionalism, which sought to escape the stigma of the irrational by removing all apparent vestiges of a rationalizing *lengua culta*— it is the discourse of alien Reason that itself constitutes the textual surface, while the presence of a local and counter-rationality is negatively embodied in the framework and constellation of the textual flow.

In *antropofagia*—the vanguard cultural "movement" launched by Oswald's second manifesto—this strategy is given a more precise and tangible configuration in the archetypal act of cannibalism. The *Manifesto* itself plays ironically on the "theory" that the Enlightenment discourse of natural right, leading from Locke through Rousseau and ultimately to the *Declaration of the Rights of Man* and the Bourgeois Revolution as such, has its origins in Montaigne's "noble savage," based on the first reports from Brazil of "cannibalism" among members of the Tupinamba tribal aggregate. The Bourgeois Revolution is only half-jokingly said to originate in the *Revolução Caraiba* (the Carib Revolution), that is, in the "revolutionary" advance to cannibalism, "the permanent transformation," in Oswald's celebrated carnivalizing of Freud, "of taboo into totem."[6] *A poesia pau-brasil* becomes the operating principle of autonomous culture by virtue of its direct, bodily incorporation of Reason, a "synthesis" that the rationalizing agency itself apparently fails to mediate: "I asked a man what Rights were. He told me they were a guarantee of the exercise of the possible. That man was named Galli Mathias. I ate him."[7]

The literary practice of *antropofagia*, amounting to little more than the manifesto and the pamphletary activities of a "Clube de Antropofagia" organized around a short-lived journal of the same name, essentially limits itself to proclaiming the new autonomy without specifying the conditions that would take it beyond the level of clever sloganizing. In 1933, after *a revolução de '30"* (the Revolution of 1930, which launched the Vargasian New State) and his embrace of Marxism, Oswald himself self-critically abjured the movement, "confessing," according to Benedito Nunes, "that he had been a clown of the bourgeoisie . . . who . . . had undertaken the vanguardist experience as a result of a poorly understood uneasiness and who was ignorant of the social origin and political basis of his feelings."[8] But modern accounts of Brazilian literary and cultural history generally compensate this moment of infantilism by crediting *antropofagia* and the general "nativist" turn of *a geração de '22* with the intellectual discovery of what was to become the formula for a new popular discourse of *cultura brasileira*, which remains dominant to this day.[9] If today modern Brazilian culture can point to the artistic success of a *Macunaíma* or a *Vidas secas*, as well as to their Cinema Novo film versions, then, as this redemptive line of interpretation goes, something of this achievement must be owed to the manifestos. These, as befits a vanguard, may be thought of as having committed a kind of exemplary aesthetic suicide while wresting a new discursive model from the captivity of neocolonial cultural dependency.

Regardless of how or whether we credit such claims, however, we may observe that what underlies the phantasmagoric operations of *antropofagia* is a formal identification of autonomy with *consumption* itself as the moment of synthesis. The impish and self-consciously transgressive mode of discourse that Oswald adopts from the European avant-garde seems in fact to work almost as a mechanism of repression against a violation of aesthetic dogma that even the *Manifesto* is not quite ready to defend: the degrading of *production* as such, of the productive agencies of rational discourse, to the level of a secondary and merely contingent factor in the synthesis of an independent cultural subject. As an emblem of autonomy, cannibalism is less important for its shock effect than for its formal correspondence to an arcane and paradoxical form of economy, or mode of production. This is a mode resting exclusively on a consumption that accomplishes in itself the socially necessary tasks of both production and reproduction. Marx refers to this abstract economic form in the first pages of the *Grundrisse* as "consumptive production."[10]

At the discursive level of *antropofagia*, consumptive production—that is, the identity of production and consumption as mediated by the latter—represents little more than the effort to outsmart rhetorically the dialectic of dependency. Nevertheless, the manifesto serves to unveil a latent logic of *circulation* at work in the ideological construction of autonomous cultural space. It now appears that the precise problem with dependency is not just that cultural goods must be brought in from the outside but that in coming from without and being locally consumed they do not give rise to a circulation *within* the local space, and thus they simply confirm the larger, extrinsic circuit of the world market. "Cultural dependency" thus describes a consumption that is severed from production. Consumption confirms the consumers themselves as subjects that are nonproductive. For there to exist even the formal possibility of a locus of autonomy upon the site of the neocolonialized culture, it must first be possible to project this space as one in which the circuit of cultural production and consumption is complete. An adequate configuration of autonomy must do more than situate the elements of synthesis—it must also establish the procedure whereby the synthesis itself gives rise to a local, self-mediating cultural economy.

The transcultural clearly conforms to this stipulation. Yet it is also vitiated by it. Against the condition of dependency—consumption at the price of production—it proposes what seems, indeed, to be the obvious remedy: an initial prohibition on direct consumption of the imported cultural product so as to enable its transfer to that regional, interior site sufficiently removed from its authoritative cultural aura to allow the transcultural incorporation to take place. Here consumption occurs, but it has now become, to borrow once more from

Marx, "productive consumption," a consumption mediated by an already dominant will to produce. Transfer of the cultural import thus amounts to its conversion into a *means of production*. The littoral walls that the cultural import must penetrate in order to be "transculturated" are thus like the walls of a factory that the commodity—whether as raw material or labor power—must penetrate in order to arrive at the point of production and set the production process itself in motion.

But what of the product itself? As the transcultural narrative, it abruptly departs from the circulatory space of its production and stands motionless, as if its mere static existence were sufficient confirmation of the autonomous cultural subject it is supposed to embody. But products do not stand still—or at least not for long—for if they do, the economy itself begins to disintegrate. The product must be consumed, whether "productively" or not, and in any case it must be transferred once more to the site of consumption. Where is this site? The transcultural model never explicitly proposes an answer here, but the evident assumption is that this site corresponds to the reader, however vaguely and abstractly construed. But, as I hope my preceding critique of transcultural theory has shown, the site, or moment, of reading does not coincide with the regional transculturating site of production. Once production has been accounted for, we remain, in fact, anchored to the site of the abstract social "reason" of capital itself, of the uniformly transparent space of the global market. In configuring itself as an effect of production—more precisely, of productive consumption—transcultural autonomy forgets that production inevitably reproduces the cleavage of presynthetic factors that prompt and condition production in the first place. The transcultural model fails to surmount the contradiction of all exoticism, however mediated, in that, however far the dominant rationality flees from its own abstraction and bad universality in the quest for a true particular, the effect of particularity is only for the rationalizing agency, only a particularity at the behest and within the spatial confines of "universal" reason.

Proceeding now in a purely speculative and somewhat allegorical mode, I might propose that in order fully to satisfy its own circulatory logic the spatial configuration of cultural autonomy must discover a means of articulating the abstract circuit of modern industrial capital without at any point permitting capital itself—that is, universalizing, alien categories of mediation—to intervene in the circulation process. From a literally economic standpoint, this is clearly an absurdity and a contradiction in terms. But to the degree that the imaginary—and, we might almost say, narrative—dimensions of the economic categories impinge upon the ideology of cultural dependency and autonomy—and, I would argue, they do in the most unmistakable fashion in the postcolonial world—the formal postulate of a local "natural" economy of cultural goods effectively conditions all attempts to "think" this problem through. The transcultural model ultimately fails to satisfy this postulate, because it is unable to specify, so to speak, a mode of consumption that can carry over and preserve the regional autonomy of its productive moment. The regional space of production fails to articulate a similar space of consumption. Thus *mexicanidad* becomes the spontaneous subject effect of a *Pedro Páramo* or of the utterance [ching — —] so long as these cultural texts themselves are poised at the moment of productive synthesis. As soon as this moment has passed—here, we are in the temporal realm of the always already—*mexicanidad* falls from its subject position. *Mexicanidad* does not consume but is itself consumed, does not mediate but is itself mediated by the abstract, prehegemonic subject of capital and state.

The particular, if as yet purely theoretical, superiority of consumptive production as the economic configuration of cultural autonomy lies in its avoidance of the spatial cleavage of production per se. To refer, again, to the *Grundrisse*,

> production is the generality, distribution and exchange the particularity, and consumption the singularity in which the whole is joined together. . . . Consumption, which is conceived not only as a terminal point but also as an end-in-itself, actually belongs outside economics except insofar as it reacts in turn upon the point of departure and initiates the whole process anew.[11]

By proposing consumption as the ideally mediating principle, Oswaldian cultural politics appears to satisfy formally the postulate of a local, self-contained circulation of cultural capital. Consuming the colonizer's civilization whole rather than "productively," the "anthropophagous" cultural agent makes his own bodily subjectivity the "end-in-itself," the purpose of cultural activity rather than just another means toward its abstract, postponed moment of production.

But then who or what is this cultural agent? Reading *antropofagia* within the ambit of Oswald's own literary practice and that of the "generation of 1922"— that is, of *modernismo* as an aesthetically vanguard practice—the question seems merely to beg itself. But discounting the claims of the avant-garde actually to carry out the cultural politics it formulates as a call to action and taking into account the developments in Brazilian aesthetic and literary culture subsequent to the political upheavals of 1930, we can perhaps read *antropofagia* as prefiguring the new status of the linguistic vernacular itself—a Brazilian Portuguese—as the very locus of cultural autonomy. Language would appear to be, formally speaking, a model practice of consumptive production by virtue of its capacity to "produce" the world by engulfing it whole. Language would not itself exist without the prior existence of an objective, nonlinguistic stratum or referent, and yet the moment at which language is still outside this stratum and poised to incorporate it is never a moment of "presence." Such incorporation is always already the case. Language's "consumption" of the world is, by virtue of its constituted being as language, already its "production" of it. The task of forging autonomy out of culture's own consumptive moment can then perhaps be more concretely engaged as the process of learning to "speak" as a single "language" the multiplicity of cultural practices that, in their mutual separation as instances of "production," fail to resist the mediating power of the colonizing circuit of (unequal) exchange. Contrary to the production of a fetishized "orality," such as that typically found in the transcultural narratives of the neoregionalists, eliciting the autonomy effect requires not the written illusion of speech but the utilization of writing in its formal capacity to provide an apparently single, monologic site for the representation of a subject whose real unity realizes itself only in the dialogic realm of successive speech acts. The narrative itself need not speak. What it must do, rather, is supply the representational conditions for the practice of a "language" that dissolves all texts—all productions—in the identity of its own process as continuous consumptive production.

It becomes illuminating, in attempting to draw out this consumptive, "dialogical" property of the larger cultural text, to contrast two of *modernismo*'s classic fictional narratives: Oswald's *Memorias sentimentais de João Miramar (1928)* and Mario de Andrade's celebrated culture-epic *Macunaíma* (1928). *João Miramar* (which claims in its fictionalized introduction to have brought Brazilian Portuguese into the twentieth century)[12] consists of an extended series of short, lexically and grammatically eccentric journal entries of the fictional *paulista* bourgeois named in the title. Putting aside the many formal curiosities of a writing that may be described as a Brazilian pastiche of Joycean prose, we may observe in Oswald's narrative a purely formal effort to impel Brazilian Portuguese out of its entrapment in the dialectic of dependency—for example, its stigmatization as a "dialect"—by producing sentences that do not obey the logic of "automatic writing" or the aleatory so much as they consistently exceed the purely discursive limits of speech. Plagued, like Miramar himself, by the shamefully archaic idiolects of outlandish *capatazes* and bombastic *doctores*, the *Memorias* can stave off threats to their own modernity only by estranging themselves from any possible spoken rearticulation. This is evidently to be achieved through continual attempts at reductive synthesis (ellipsis) and the introduction of neologisms.[13] Thus, contrary to the logic of his own cutural program, as promulgated in *Pau-brasil* and *Antropofagia*, Oswald applies in *João Miramar* the principles of a radically productionist circuit of autonomy. One can hardly even speak here of a transcultural productive consumption; it is rather a production ex nihilo, production as a purely abstract and spiritual redemption from the curse of a consumption that, like that of the *cafezeiros*, bespeaks a cultural vacuum.

Macunaíma, on the other hand—long since enshrined as veritable Ur-text of modern *cultura brasileira*—owes its popular as well as critical canonization to what may be described as a literal, if ironic, adherence to the principles of *antropofagia*. In telling the story of Macunaíma "o heroi sem nenhum caracter," the narrative text makes no initial attempt to foreground its own formal autonomy. Instead it adopts the formal conventions of the ethnographic texts—Koch-

Grünbergs's collections of tribal legends from the Orinoco region—from which much of the folkloric material is drawn. What we read in *Macunaíma* is, from a generic standpoint, simply the fictionalized speech of an *informant* as it is recorded and appropriated by the rational apparatus of ethnography. The exotic and childlike manner of the narrative's horizontal movement, for all its charm and wit, is at all times *formally* consistent with the traditional rationalizing hierarchy (*civilización* vs. *barbarie*) that foregrounds the narrative itself as vertically linked to a "culture" in the most abject state of dependence and heteronomy.

In adopting the formal, generic arrangement of the ethnographic frame, however, the narrative gradually sets about violating the rules of rational ethnographic procedure: it exceeds the spatiotemporal logic of the field, or mapping, principle according to which the speech of the informant loses interpretive value as soon as it begins to show signs of exogenous cultural influences. In this sense, the cultural syncretism represented by the central figure of Macunaíma—a black, born into an Amerindian tribal kin group, who proceeds to turn white, travel to São Paulo, operate machines, and so on—goes beyond the mere allegorization of modern Brazilian culture.

Macunaíma seeks to undermine the very categories of an estranging, ethnographizing Reason—race, natural environment, level of technical development, and such—whereby cultural domination is made to appear rational. Macunaíma, not only as allegorical hero but as a "Brazilian" *parole* articulated through the device of the informant, spills over into a spatial and historical domain before the "civilizing" agency that inhabits it has time to react with its array of rationalizing cultural codes. In true anthropophagistic fashion, an apparently domesticated cultural subject trumps its more powerful opponent by feigning a retreat. The speech of the informant, accepted by the ethnographer as an index of the compliance and controlled scientific mediation of the "savage" subject, succeeds in ironizing this naively positivist creed by leaving no doubt as to the informant's worldliness. More than this, however, it performs the even wilier feat of appropriating the entire discursive field—of passing unnoticeably from the level of a series of speech acts interpreted as meaningful only within a controlled, rationally delimited field to the level of discourse as such, with the power to deploy its own spatial codes. *Cultura brasileira* outflanks the logic of its marginality and unreason, taking advantage of Reason's own temporary silence—the frame, the moment of objectification—in order to "speak," that is, reencode this Reason as simply another of its own infinitely variable representations. Thus Macunaíma's favorite and oft-repeated remark—"Que preguiça!"—not only "proves" that he, or the informant, has read Paulo Prado's *Retrato do Brasil*[14] but invites speculation that all such texts, however vainly they may insist on their own "scientific" detachment, are really nothing more than the same *pensée sauvage* that they deludedly believe they have domesticated.

In *Macunaíma*, then, cultural autonomy takes shape as the incessant narrative *consumption* of dominant cultural categories, borne along by an already discoursing subject. Synthesis occurs "consumptively," by a simple procedure of extending beyond "rational" limits an operation—the incorporation of modern reality into a popular Brazilian speech idiom—that is not in itself external to the historical and economic condition of dependency. As *consumptive production*, the cultural discourse of *Macunaíma* starts out from this real space of circulation as it necessarily exists for an economically "dependent" subject. *João Miramar*, on the other hand, must seek to arrest the movement of discourse in order to propose as its own model of synthesis a species of neologistic contraption. Oswald's narrative must first climb outside of what it perceives as the merely formal, abstract space of dependency so as to represent the equally abstract and negative space of autonomy. But it does so only to discover itself at last unable to reenter the space it has evacuated. True to its avant-garde principles, *João Miramar* takes on the abstract autonomy of its productive apparatus by taking itself off the market altogether. It thereby assures that the circumstances of its consumption, and thereby its moment of cultural realization, will be all the more rigidly determined by abstract market forces.

3. Cinema Novo: Consumptive Production and the Industrial Avant-Garde

The short, densely written episodes of *João Miramar* (numbered 1 through 163) have suggested to more than one critic the cinematic technique of montage. Is this simply another sign of Oswald's juvenile obeisance to the imported European vanguard, shortly to be overcome in the ruptural ecstacy of *pau-brasil* and *antropofagia*? The conclusion may seem warranted, but once again the dialectic is not so clean as this: for Oswald's novel is also, in a fleeting way, the story, and not simply the formal mimicking, of filmmaking. In episodes 101 and 102 we find *João Miramar*'s eponymous hero embarked on the career of a *grande industrial* as chief stockholder in the Piaçagüera Lightning and Famous Company Pictures of São Paulo and Around. The venture is short-lived, however. By episode 120 ("Ultimo Film"), it has collapsed in bankruptcy, causing the loss of the considerable family fortune that João, "fazendeiro matrimonial," had inherited thanks to a fortunate marriage. The result of this fiasco is, in a sense, the novel itself: a failure as a film producer, Miramar resigns himself to the writing of his memoirs.

The history of Brazilian film enterprise is fairly accurately reflected in this otherwise unremarkable subplot. Film historians Randal Johnson and Robert Stam, for example, recount how in 1911 a veritable *bela época* of local independent filmmaking, which had its beginnings as early as 1900 in Brazil, ended with the sudden influx of North American films and film business. "The foreign film," they write,

became the standard by which all films were to be judged, thus rendering problematic the exhibition of the less technically polished Brazilian product. Since local distributors lacked the infrastructural organization possessed by foreign distributors, the internal market began to function for the benefit of the industrial products from abroad. . . . The Brazilian market became a tropical appendage of the North American market.[15]

Had the hapless João launched his venture some fifty years later, however, the results might have been different. The mid 1950s mark the beginning of the independent filmmaking movement known as Cinema Novo. Although its earliest products are mainly low-budget artisanal films that played to small audiences, the efforts of Cinema Novo, in combination with the Brazilian state, resulted by the 1970s in the rebirth of a native film industry. Created by the Brazilian government in the late 1960s and later strengthened by Geisel appointee Roberto Farias (of Cinema Novo reputation), *Embrafilme* becomes the principal coproducer and distributor of Brazilian films, many of them directed by former Cinema Novo directors or their disciples. Under the umbrella of *Embrafilme* not only do locally made films command a certain preallotted share of the national market; some, like Bruno Barreto's *Dona Flor and Her Two Husbands* and other Sonia Braga spectacles, become lucrative exports. Although the sheer economic mass of Hollywood imports still weighs heavily on the Brazilian market, the Brazilian film industry commands an autonomy that is unique in Latin America (only the Cuban film industry can begin to compare).

This outcome is, in its way, entirely consistent with the aesthetics of consumptive production. For despite the illusions fostered by an authorial fetishism, the filmmaking process turns, by its very logic of production, on the moment of consumption. Here we may simply follow Walter Benjamin in his radical defense of the film in "The Work of Art in the Age of Mechanical Reproduction." In its most concise dialectical summation of Benjamin's initially optimistic projection of auratic decay, the essay makes the following argument:

Mechanical reproduction of art changes the reaction of the masses toward art. The reactionary attitude toward a Picasso painting changes into the progressive reaction toward a Chaplin movie. The progressive reaction is characterized by the direct, intimate fusion of visual enjoyment with the orientation of the expert. Such fusion is of great social significance. The greater the decrease in the social significance of an art form, the sharper the distinction between criticism and enjoyment by the public. The conventional is uncritically enjoyed, and the truly new is criticized with aversion. With regard to the screen, the critical and the receptive attitudes of the public coincide.[16]

Transposing Bejamin's category of reception, his essay can itself be read as propounding a "consumptive production" as the newly exposed site of a postauratic aesthetic autonomy. A film, unlike a painting, incorporates into its very synthesis as a *work* the new and legitimate demand of the urban masses to "bring things 'closer' spatially and humanly."[17] The collective agencies that produce the film have become fully secondary and contingent upon the synthetic moment that Benjamin elsewhere, in reference to architecture, denotes as "tactile appropriation." The latter is characterized by its complete relinquishment of traditional auratic contemplation in preference for a gradual and habituated mastery of contents that Benjamin refers to as "distraction." "Reception in a state of distraction . . . finds in the film its true means of exercise."[18]

Benjamin's utopian prognosis for what we might simply call the "Picasso/Chaplin dialectic" finds here a peculiar inflection—not merely as an argument for *modernismo* on film but as the general propensity for the contemporary Brazilian avant-garde to embrace the spectrum of new technical media (including radio and television) as the heretofore missing link in a frustrated quest for mass-cultural mediation.[19]

And, not coincidentally, the wedding of avant-garde and mechanical reproduction finds perhaps its classic Brazilian instance in the film version of the novel *Macunaíma*. Made by Cinema Novo director Joaquim Pedro de Andrade and released in 1969, *Macunaíma* is credited with having given Cinema Novo its first decisive box office success. It casts Grande Otelo, star of the *chanchada* (popular musical film) in the title role and favors the slapstick comedy of this genre as a filmic equivalent for the festive vernacular of the original text. The obscure, mytho-allegorical characters are rendered as more recognizable types, drawn from contemporary events (Ci, "mãe da mata," becomes an urban guerrilla, and so forth). Following in the path of Leon Hirzman's *Garota de Ipanema*, the film is made in color, foregoing the Cinema Novo's typically austere preference for black-and-white.[20]

Despite the homage paid to Mario in the selection of the text, however, Joaquim Pedro's theoretical debt is openly declared as belonging to Oswald. In a note accompanying the film's international premiere at the Venice Film Festival, the director invokes *antropofagia* as "an exemplary mode of consumerism adopted by underdeveloped peoples. *Macunaíma* is the story of a Brazilian devoured by Brazil."[21] Still, rediscovery of the 1928 manifesto is not without critical intent. In a 1966 interview with Alex Viany, Joaquim Pedro had, for instance, proclaimed:

All of us in Brazil—authors of films, books, plays—continually receive information from the cultural vanguard throughout the world. We are obviously affected by this information. There is always a degree of interpenetration and communication between the intelligentsia of more developed and less developed countries. This phenomenon is a perennial one. The modernists of 1922, for example, attempted to deal with this problem by rejecting all imported values and techniques not relevant to our reality in favor of authentically Brazilian processes that would be, in principle, communicative and unalienating. The works produced by this movement, according to this rationale, should have had a greater degree of communication than they in fact had. Despite the good intentions of their program, the movement's complex intellectual processes and intellectual pretension made such communication impossible. We would do well to re-examine the movement of 1922 in terms of the present situation.[22]

Consumptive production, in other words, remains theoretically valid, but it has been flawed in practice. While conceding his centrality, it failed to establish any real contact with the Brazilian mass consumer. Extrapolating Joaquim Pedro's criticism, we can observe that whereas the original *Macunaíma* sacrifices the vanguard autonomy of the signifier in the interests of a popular individual whose right to consume is recognized in the text's colloquial Brazilian register, its actual consumption is prohibited by the text's own restricted circulation as a literary commodity. It continues to circulate within an elite cultural discourse that has refined its own concept through a "popularization" but that keeps the masses themselves at arm's length. Meanwhile the film version is "formally innovative, politically radical, *and* immensely popular with the Brazilian masses." It "radicalizes ideological positions latent in the novel, just as Cinema Novo radicalizes and takes to their ultimate conclusions many issues first raised by the Modernist movement."[23]

Students of Critical Theory will certainly recall at this point Adorno's notorious reception of "The Work of Art in the Age of Mechanical Reproduction." In a letter to Benjamin, Adorno sharply attacked the "Picasso/Chaplin dialectic" for its "romanticization" of the mass (proletarian) consumer and concomitant refusal of a dialectic of technique to the "autonomous work of art." Both Picasso and Chaplin, both "high" and "low," in Adorno's words, "bear the stigmata of capitalism . . . Both are torn halves of an integral freedom, to which, however, they do not add up."[24]

In thus formulating a critical position against what might be termed Benjamin's tendencies to an aesthetic populism, Adorno initiates a line of critique that is ultimately to become a general assault on a mass-mediated art, tagged with the rubric the "culture industry." I shall assume, in what follows, a general familiarity with this criticism—as expounded primarily in Adorno and Horkhiemer's *Dialectic of Enlightenment*—but the suggestive metaphor of the "torn halves" can be read as containing its gist: if the "mass consumability" of the Chaplin film and the revolutionized perceptual apparatus of the Picasso painting do not "add up" to the "integral freedom" that Benjamin envisions, this is because the very social space within which this—as Adorno admits—eminently desirable synthesis ought to be realized is absent. Or, to put it in historicist terms, the space of integral freedom is envisioned too late. It has already been usurped by a more radical integration of exclusive character.

The usurper is the commodity per se—that "integral unfreedom" that, as the bearer to an ever-increasing degree of *all* social mediation, as society itself in its subjective moment, leaves behind no burrow or niche for an autonomy of human dimension. Given this, it becomes the task of the culture industry to supply an ideological legitimacy, to preserve the myth of an "integral freedom," of a continuity between "high" and "low," when none in fact exists. Construed in the terms of natural economy, culture industry can be equated with the return of "productive consumption" to abolish the remaining autonomous spheres of "consumptive production." Culture industry gives rise to a "cultural commodity" that, in being consumed, sustains the appearance of autonomy while in essence it abolishes it utterly. "The consumer becomes the ideology of the pleasure industry, whose institutions he cannot escape."[25] The existence of the "cultural commodity" is witness to the fact that consumption itself has become reified abstraction. Culture merely adds the ideological effect, the human "aura" of a consumption that is purely an economic reflex. Thus the cultural commodity, as a special kind of ware, logically posits the cultural subject while simultaneously canceling its truth. Culture seems finally to come into its own as a mass democratic phenomenon—the myth of populism—at precisely the moment of its total demise. In becoming a mass-mediated sphere, it severs the last bond that tied it to something genuinely human and emancipatory. What democratizes culture—its commodification—is what finally dispenses with it.

The Brazilian cultural politics that simply affirms the joining of the "torn halves" through the autonomous operation of a consumptive production would seem, on its surface, to call forth precisely this line of criticism. What, it may be thought, is the supposed synthesis of a Cinema Novo *Macunaíma*, for all its vaunted radicalism, but the forerunner of *Dona Flor* and other *Embrafilme* commercialized exoticisms, not to mention Brazil's immense television dream factory and the specialized culture industry of *carnaval*? The Adornian suspicion may be readily formulated that *antropofagia*'s transfer of autonomy to culture's *consumptive* moment is a simple ruse, concealing what is already the anticipated industrialization, ergo abdication, of the avant-garde.

Such is the conclusion suggested by the contemporary Brazilian critic Roberto Schwarz, whose cultural criticism I now wish to turn to in some detail. Schwarz is Adorno's student, and thus naturally the bearer of some "influence," but what will matter to us here is both the question of the adequacy of Adornian Critical Theory to Brazilian culture and Schwarz's possibly transcultural application of it. The specter of a Brazilian culture industry is thus, for example, explicitly conjured in Schwarz's 1967 "Nota sobre vanguarda e conformismo." The occasion is a 1957 interview with four Brazilian composers who, in an obviously Oswaldian declaration of faith, had announced their intention to produce compositions for the commercial market. "Participation of the masses . . . unites the two stages of the process: you end up not knowing when production ends and consumption begins; it's all just the same thing—to produce consuming, to consume producing."[26] Schwarz is careful to reconstruct the Benjaminian standpoint that the composers appear to adopt. But is it the actual social transcendence of the commodity form—"the virtual presence of socialism"—that is envisioned in this rejection of artisanal composition or simply the circumstance that the artisanal product "doesn't sell"? Consumptive production, so long as its practice is determined by the boundaries of the commodity form, is at best the formula for a pseudoautonomy, at worst nothing but a rationale for an expansion of the market and "the good royalities."

> "It's all just the same thing" calls to mind "Brazil is just one big family." And the reciprocity of the final formula—to produce consuming and to consume producing—obfuscates the mediation of capital, which consists precisely in separating consumption and production. . . . The artist forges the link between capital and consumption.[27]

This emergent critique of Brazilian culture industry is carried yet further in Schwarz's brilliant 1969 essay, "Culture e Política, 1964–1969." Here Schwarz describes how, in the period following the military takeover and the effective decapitation of the populist political regime, the position of the left avant-garde nevertheless remains intact. "There exists a relative cultural hegemony of the left in the country."[28] Its activities evidently pose no real threat to capital, unlike those of the popular cultural movements in Pernambuco and Rio, which had actually begun the process of organizing masses of workers and peasants through agitational theater and literacy campaigns and which were immediately suppressed by the generals. The "revenge of the provinces," in the form of a sudden wave of petit bourgeois philistinism and nostalgia for the prepopulist period, is finally unable to unseat the reigning left intelligentsia. The result of their collision Schwarz detects in the increasingly ironic and allegorical recourse to anachronism that typifies the new avant-garde inflection referred to above in the context of *Macunaíma*, namely, *tropicalismo*. But unlike Pedro Joaquim and the celebrants of a purportedly radicalized *modernismo*, Schwarz rejects the empirical claims made for *tropicalismo*'s technically mediated "critical success." His reasoning here does not entail the conservatively modernist defense of the hermetically autonomous work per se, however, but rather the exposure of the romanticization inherent in the Benjaminian/tropicalist postulate of an autonomous and "critical" subject situated, in theory, at the pole of consumption/reception.

Such mass consumption is not, as the tropicalists are inclined to think, an index of "critical enjoyment" on the part of the public but, to use Schwarz's phrase, a *snobismo de masas*, that is, a mere consumption of the *aura* of the *novos meios*, unconcerned with any radical message insinuated into the commercial packaging. Against the Benjaminian/tropicalist faith in a "fusion" of enjoyment and critical expertise, Schwarz proposes to uncover a process of integration based solely on the consumer's sense of inadequacy and backwardness before a *modernidade* that mesmerizes him.

> Before the tropicalist image, before the apparently surreal incongruency that results from the described combination, the tuned-in spectator will reach for the obvious buzz words: Brazil is incredible, he'll say, it's cool, it's the living end, it's too much. By means of these expressions, in which sympathy and disgust are indiscernible, he affiliates himself to the group of those who have the "sense" of the national character.[29]

The effect of such consumption is only to reproduce the original fissure between mass and avant-garde, between underdevelopment and modernity, since the consumer's linkage to "the new," like that of the underdeveloped social formation itself, "is brought about as the structural outcome of his social backwardness, which gets reproduced rather than extinguished."[30]

The thrust of Schwarz's criticism of the Brazilian cultural vanguard here and elsewhere is to liquidate the premise, basic to the avant-garde since the manifestos of Oswald, that the consumptive production of culture on the part of the masses can outflank the heteronomy of dependency where an aesthetics of production fails to do so. The context governing much of Schwarz's critique is, as may be obvious, the attack on populism and its train of illusions—among them the theory of an emancipatory industrialization of modernist culture—which are seen, and rightly so, as greatly responsible for the disaster of 1964. Developments in the 1970s and 1980s, particularly the parallel phenomena of an intellectual and cultural *abertura* (opening) and the unceasing immiseration and oppression of the Brazilian masses even as their "culture" is marketed by powerfully entrenched industrial mechanisms, certainly speak to the acuity of Schwarz's then-unpopular Adornian pessimism.

But I cannot help observing how, in the course of this Brazilian "repetition" of one of Critical Theory's most notorious theoretical disputes, certain subtle conceptual inversions and elisions are entailed. For here it must be recalled that the Culture Industry functions within Adornian critical discourse not simply as an empirical concept—though it surely is this—but also as a logical and aesthetic pole in the dialectic of the modern, autonomous work of art. If the culture industry represents the absolute hegemony of the commodity form over previously independent spheres of art and culture, it is the autonomous work of art that, by virtue of its complete severance from all mechanisms of social exchange, its vaunted nonfungibility, embodies the opposing principle, the very object and meaning of Adornian cultural politics. Adorno's defense of modernism and the avant-garde follows strictly from what is, a priori, conceived as their absolute subservience, however blind, to the principle of artistic autonomy and the laws of immanent aesthetic form.

In Brazil, however, it is precisely the avant-garde that, governed by the impulse to cultural and artistic autonomy, ultimately arrives at an aesthetic of industrialization. Culture industry, despite the political and economic dangers it entails, comes to represent, on the level of vanguard aesthetic and cultural theory, the social embodiment of consumptive production, ergo autonomy. Culture industry here ceases, in a purely formal sense, to occupy the site of that which is to be negated in a dialectic giving way to the autonomous work. Nor is it simply the end point of a Benjaminian dialectic of technical emancipation. It represents, rather, the final unfolding—the negation of the negation—of the autonomy principle per se.

"The artist forges the link." Here Schwarz has aptly exposed the hidden commodity logic of electronic *antropofagia*. What his Adornian reasoning fails to reveal, however, is what we may describe only somewhat ironically as the "utopianizing" of the commodity space itself. For, in the discourse of consumptive production, it is precisely the commodity that becomes the imaginary site of an autochthonous self-mediating cultural subjectivity.

Here we must again be reminded that in Adornian cultural and aesthetic theory the commodity is prefigured as an absolutely hermetic, interiorized space, impervious to any genuinely human and autonomous agency. It is this space that then is to find its utopian Other in the equally hermetic interior of the modernist work of art. Presupposed in this one-dimensional logic, however, is the possibility of a vantage point *outside*—"over and against"—a commodity thereby endowed with a quality of stable and exteriorized evidence. Adornian modernism can initially posit itself as the concrete, emancipatory negation of the commodity fetish for the sole reason that it beholds the commodity from this vantage point. This, in economic terms, is the vantage point from which the circuit of industrial capital (as in volume 2 of *Capital*) appears as a visible unity, allowing the commodity itself to take shape as a discrete and integral phase of capital. The circuit of modern industrial capital, even if it has become global in scope, centers in the metropolis, where production (that is, capitalist production) mediates consumption absolutely—hence the apparently monolithic guise of the culture industry and the impenetrability of the commodity abstraction. A properly metropolitan modernism, theorized as the specifically aesthetic self-consciousness of this economic vantage point, implies the outward, positive evidence of the abstract commodity form as a phase in the circulation of capital. Thus it is not merely unhindered circulation—the free movement of commodities—that is here presupposed but precisely the subjective standpoint that can regard the time-space contained in this movement as empty and undifferentiated.

But we can argue that in the modern, imperialized periphery it is just this exteriority and evidence of the commodity that is withheld. The commodity, although not precisely an absence, situates itself outside the economic subject as a surrounding horizon. The periphery is "de-centered" with respect to the circuit of capital in its totality of discrete phases. It enters the circulation process at the site of one (or more) of its phases (L [labor], MP [means of production], and C [commodity] in Marx's formula in volume 2 *Capital*)[31] but not at the site of the circuit as a whole. Autonomy cannot, as a result, seek its configuration as an anticommodity—as the dialectical negation of the commodity in its integral relation to the totality of economic relations—because the movement of commodities is not itself autonomous from the standpoint of the periphery. The time-space of circulation is ruptured and infested with historical negativity. Thus it does not make conceptually or ideologically available the "inhuman abstraction" against which the modern, autonomous work is posed in a movement of dialectical negation.

Perhaps it is for this reason that Schwarz's Adornian critique of Brazilian modernism in its industrial and "Benjaminian" moment neglects to propose an aesthetic to put in the place of the industrial vanguard. Schwarz refuses consumptive production as merely a clever pseudosynthesis, equipped, like the discourse of populism, to conceal the fact of class division. Yet he declines the return to a more orthodox, "productionist," and pre-Oswaldian modernism. Autonomy is not, evidently, something to be simply squeezed back into the formal immanence of the *work*. Where, then, is it to be situated?

Schwarz's only critical approbation in "Cultura e Política" is granted, almost in passing, to a handful of Cinema Novo films: Pereira dos Santos's *Vidas Secas* (1963), Glauber Rocha's *Deus e Diabo na Terra do Sol* (1964), and Rui Guerra's *Os Fuzis* (1964). All are from the movement's pretropicalist, first phase, which ends with the 1964 coup, and are associated by Schwarz with Rocha's retrospective proclamation in 1965 of "uma estética da fome"—"an aesthetic of hunger," or, as it is sometimes translated, "an aesthetic of violence."[32] Schwarz pointedly and favorably contrasts these films' supposed subordination of technique to a specifically radical political content with *tropicalismo*'s technical self-referentiality.

Rocha's reference to *fome* has typically been understood as pertaining both to the subject matter of most of the Cinema Novo films of this period—the oppression of Brazil's urban and rural poor, particularly the northeastern *sertanejo*—and to their characteristically sparse and rough-hewn editing and cinematography. Thus the "hunger" of the characters—Fabiano, Vitoria, and their children in *Vidas Secas*, for example—is emphatically reinforced by its appearance of governing the movement of the camera itself. Periods of, by Hollywood standards, excessive stasis, such as the much-noted death scene of the family dog, are coupled with episodes in which the camera moves violently and erratically. This, as Johnson and Stam put it,

> serves as a warning to the spectator not to expect the fast pacing and density of incident that characterizes most fiction films. The spectator's experience, in short, will be as dry as that of the protagonists. The relative fidelity to the tempo and duration of peasant life forms part of the film's meaning.[33]

Alongside and as part of these specifically filmic procedures, however, it is impossible to ignore the implicitly critical impact of *fome* on the aesthetics of *antropofagia*. In conformity with the principle of consumptive production, the *fome* films foreground and privilege the moment of consumption; it is the consumer, not the producer, who makes possible the act of cultural synthesis. But two decisive transformations have taken place.

First, the act of consuming, without ceasing to occupy the foreground, has become a moment of negativity. Consumption must take place; and yet there is nothing substantial there to consume. The consumer seeks an ideological integration in the act of consumption but is inhibited by the absence of any cultural content that does not itself beg the question of exactly who consumes. This, as Schwarz makes clear, is the question that *tropicalismo* and the populist industrial vanguard must necessarily exclude.

The second transformation entailed in the transition of *antropofagia* into *fome* is the *aesthetic formalization* of the consumptive principle as such. Films such as *Vidas Secas* and *Deus e Diabo* avoid, ideally, the uncritical, co-opting synthesis described by Schwarz as *snobismo de masas* by literally constructing *on film* the features of a radicalized, nonpopulist *preconsumer*. The *fome* film presents itself to the spectator in a condition of, as it were, predigestion, which, in theory at least, will resist the populist/tropicalist appropriation. This predigestive or auto-consumptive maneuver is most readily observable in Rocha's films, including the supposedly tropicalist *Terra em Transe* and *Antonio-das-Mortes*. The effect generated in these films is that of a radical and essentially anarchic preemption of any possible populist cultural encodement. Viewing them, one has the definite sensation of seeing something as it was, literally, not intended to be seen. The process of estrangement clearly owes something to Brecht (particularly, as Schwarz notes approvingly, in *Os Fuzis*), but the critical *detachment* of the public is less the objective than its *supplantation* by purely filmic mechanisms of reception. Consumption, in a state not of distraction but of frenzy, *assumes the position of the filmic signifier per se*—or so a semiotic reading might infer.

Here, then, is the site in question. The aesthetic autonomy that Schwarz's Adornian critique implicitly attributes to the *fome* film retains its content as consumptive production while, at the same time, it becomes a formal constituent of the work. The work's negative properties have thus retrieved their lost immanence. And yet this negativity bypasses any dialectical link to consumption as obeying the exclusive, abstract logic of exchange. The dialectic here points, rather, to a given, conjuncturally determined practice of consumption—*snobismo de masas*—that epitomizes Brazil's modernist culture industry. Negation takes the form of a preemption and displacement, rather than the more dialectically orthodox inversion. For there is no possibility here of transcending the world of commodities by a simple maneuver on the level of what is already a terrain of economic abstraction. The maneuver must be executed within the spatial coordinates of commodity relations themselves—for as long, at least, as these relations are enforced by the fact of dependent imperialist integration. The ideal of *fome* is to produce the paradoxical cultural commodity that only the nonconsumer—the one forcibly excluded *as a consumer* from the global circuit of capital and representing, in all probability, the huge majority of the world's population—might somehow have consumed.

The "aesthetic of hunger" projects, we might then say, a consumption of counterhegemonic subjects, while the consumerism associated with Brazilian industrial culture itself operates hegemonically in the interests of the ruling, propertied elites. This, in fact, is the explicit basis for Schwarz's consistently critical stance toward the "left cultural hegemony" of 1964–69—a hegemony that, one can argue, is reenthroned in the course of the *abertura* of the late 1970s. The paradox of such an arrangement is dispelled in the discovery that the same bourgeois-utopian discourse of "Brazilian-ness" that operated as the unifying ideology of pre-1964 populism continues to do so under the altered political conditions of military and "postmilitary" rule. The difference here—and this is Schwarz's great critical insight—is that where the populist projection of hegemonic space entailed the expansion of the unchallenged modernity of the urban political center to include the urban and rural masses and to exclude the older centers of rural oligarchical power, the postpopulist (and perhaps, in this particular sense, postmodernist) conjuncture finds the center itself invaded and split by the "revenge of the provinces." The populist hegemonic strategy simply proves too threatening to the dominant sectors of Brazilian capital. The result, following Schwarz, is the sudden dismemberment of the dominant ideology of the modern per se. In its place there arises the *disparate* (absurd, nonsensical), the blatant anachronism and baroque pseudosophistication of *tropicalismo*. *Modernidade* now must reappear as simply the effect, the "aura" of the one vestige of the old modernist culture that has survived intact—its industrial and electronic technification. (We cannot help but be reminded here of the very similar cultural phenomenon of North American high tech during Reaganism's "revenge of the provinces.") Having lost its uniform representationality as a modern—that is, hegemonizing—national space, "Brasil" must reinscribe itself as simply the aura of its cultural commodities.

Contrast this to the hegemonic mapping of national space that I discussed in the case of Rulfo and modern postrevolutionary Mexico. What appears as the organic and spontaneous efflux of *mexicanidad* in Rulfian narrative is historically conditional upon the hegemonizing activity of the state through its cultural institutions (education, for example) and its conquest of a regional space that threatens cultural disarticulation and subnational autonomy. There must be one *mexicanidad*, not many, and it must reflect in this oneness the institutional integrity of the state as center of political power.

What appears as an organic and spontaneous efflux of *cultura brasileira* in, let us say, an *Embrafilme* production such as *Dona Flor*, however, no longer depends exclusively on the integrity of the political-cultural state institution with its typical deployment of a single hegemonic discourse of national identity. Here the state, or hegemonic center, takes shape as the very unified space within which the cultural capital circulates. *Cultura brasileira* names not only the product but the consumer, uniting them both in a special abstract commodity substance. "Brasil," independent of what is still no doubt its precarious status as a discourse of political hegemony, gains a degree of *commercial* hegemony such that this commodity substance remains "Brasil" throughout the entire circulation process. "Brasil" becomes synonymous with the aura of its cultural goods, in the sense that its *preconsumption* of their specific contents (the same preconsumption opposed and counterposed by *fome*) sets up a second-order relation in which only the "Brazilian-ness" of the product need by appropriated. This is Schwarz's *snobismo de masas*. What is described here is essentially identical to the phenomenon of aura in such dominant consumer commodities as automobiles and soft drinks. Here even the alienated, exchange-dominated use value effectively ceases to motivate consumption, so that one consumes instead the brand; one consumes *consumption in general*, and only secondarily a use value. The key distinction of "Brasil" as the aura, rather than the general signified, of its cultural objects lies in the fact that aura performs here a directly hegemonizing function and not merely a reproductive one.

I conclude by posing a final question: Is this hegemonic "supplement" in reality merely supplemental? Does not the "crisis in hegemony" that prevails in Brazil as throughout the Latin-American imperialized periphery—the reality that no discourse, however remote from the "instrumentalized" sphere of the world, can elude hegemonic articulation—render visible what is hidden in the posthegemonic conditions of the center? I refer here to a possible congruence of the "interior" space of the *work* with a prefigured, "exterior" space of hegemonic unity. Do not, finally, the aesthetic works that form the empirical basis for the Adornian radical defense of modernism refuse to reveal this congruence only, perhaps, because this figural space has become ideologically indistinguishable from the real space of hegemonic state power?

Notes

Notes

Introduction

1. See Georg Lukács, "Expressionism: Its Significance and Decline," in *Essays on Realism* trans. David Fernbach, ed. Rodney Livingstone (Cambridge, Mass.: MIT Press, 1980), pp. 76–113.

2. Georg Lukács, "The Ideology of Modernism," in *The Meaning of Contemporary Realism*, trans. John and Necke Mander (London: Merlin Press, 1963) pp. 17–46.

In speaking of an "extra-aesthetic" modernism, I do not imply the now-frequent amplification of modernism to include all Western thought from roughly the Enlightenment through Nietzsche—as, e.g, in Habermas and others. Lukács's mapping—according to which the origins of modernism are to be sought in Western Europe following the revolutions of 1848—is retained here, but with the difference in perspective already discussed.

3. See Karl Marx, *Grundrisse*, trans. Martin Nicolaus (New York: Vintage Books, 1973), esp. pp. 440–471.

4. This is not to suggest that modernism and the avant-garde are in all cases collapsible terms. Peter Bürger, in *Theory of the Avant-Garde* (trans. Michael Shaw [Minneapolis: University of Minnesota Press, 1984]), has argued for a fundamental distinction between a modernism founded on a theory and practice of "autonomy" and an (historical) avant-garde that dedicates itself precisely to exploding "autonomy" and aims to "reintegrate art into the praxis of life" (p. 22). Bürger credits the early twentieth-century avant-garde with enabling the general cognition of "art as institution." Without denying the significance of this difference—too often ignored in contemporary art and literary history—we must nevertheless observe that the avant-garde retains from modernism a theory/practice of the "work" as social/historical agency, even if the tag of "art" is refused and the catalytic non-permanence of the "work" is propounded. And Bürger himself is the first to concede the "historical fact that the avant-garde movement did not put an end to the production of works of art, and that the social institution that is art proved resistant to the avant-gardiste attack" (p. 57). This is revealed with particular poignancy in the contemporary practice of what Bürger calls the "neo-avant-garde" (and what might as well be termed "postmodernism"): "Since now the protest of the historical avant-

garde against art as institution is accepted as *art*, the gesture of the neo-avant-garde becomes inauthentic'' (p. 53).

5. Jean-François Lyotard, "The Postmodern Condition" [excerpt] in *After Philosophy: End or Transformation?*, ed. Kenneth Baynes, James Bohman, and Thomas McCarthy (Cambridge, Mass.: MIT Press, 1987), p. 80.

6. See Richard Rorty, "Pragmatism and Philosophy," in *After Philosophy*, pp. 21–66.

7. Fredric Jameson, Introduction to *The Postmodern Condition*, by Jean-François Lyotard, trans. Geoff Bennington and Brian Massumi (Minneapolis: University of Minnesota Press, 1984)

8. Lyotard, *The Postmodern Condition*, p. 66.

9. Ibid.

10. This assessment is shared by at least two readers of *Hegemony and Socialist Strategy*, one highly critical, the other largely approving. The latter, Stanley Aronowitz in "Theory and Socialist Strategy" (*Social Text* 16 [Winter 1986/1987]: 1–16), writes that *Hegemony and Socialist Strategy* is "the boldest, if not the first attempt to marshal the entire corpus of French poststructuralist philosophy as methodological and epistemological critiques of historical materialism" (p. 1). The former reader, Ellen Meiksins Wood, in her splendid work *The Retreat from Class* (London: Verso, 1986), describes *Hegemony and Socialist Strategy* as "beautifully paradigmatic, summing up and taking to their ultimate conclusions all the NTS [New 'True' Socialist] themes, revealing with particular clarity all the slippages and contradictions, both theoretical and political, inherent in its logic" (p.47). (The New 'True' Socialists are, for Wood, the Althusserian and post-Althusserian Marxists, including Poulantzas, Hindness and Hirst, and Laclau and Mouffe, who have rejected all claims that socialism and the working class are necessarily linked.) Readers of *The Retreat from Class* will find many of Wood's conclusions about *Hegemony and Socialist Strategy* echoed in my argument.

11. Ernesto Laclau and Chantal Mouffe, *Hegemony and Socialist Strategy: Towards a Radical Democratic Politics* (London: Verso, 1985), pp. 14–15, 18; hereafter cited as *HSS*.

12. Eduard Bernstein, quoted in *HSS*, p. 33.

13. See, for example, the chapter section entitled "The Last Redoubt of Essentialism: The Economy" (*HSS*, pp. 75–85), where Laclau and Mouffe proceed from a critique of Marxian "economism" to the "discovery" that "there is no logical connection between positions in the relations of production and the mentality of the producers" (*HSS*, pp. 84–85).

14. See Wood, *The Retreat from Class*, p. 59.

15. That, in the end, Laclau and Mouffe's polemic against "essentialism" functions as a smoke screen for their total embrace of philosophical idealism cannot fail to escape the attention of the careful reader of *Hegemony and Socialist Strategy*. This is, in a sense, one of the virtues of the work vis-à-vis the more clouded and eclectic approach taken, for example, in Lyotard's "language game" empiricism. The assumption throughout *Hegemony and Socialist Strategy* is that materialism is *ipso facto* essentialism, i.e., a belief in the *fixity* of objects external to consciousness or "discourse." That dialectical materialism, as methodologically applied by Marx and openly expounded by Engels and Lenin, affirms the primacy of material, social being over consciousness *at the same time* that it denies any *fixed* essence to material objects and insists on the processive, dynamic flux of reality, is a fact widely known even to Marxism's traditional philosophical opponents. It is scarcely credible that Laclau and Mouffe are ignorant of this philosophical line, whatever they may think of it; yet the theoretical core of their work rests upon what I can describe only as a systematic refusal to confront it. Thus, in the key section of chapter 3 of *Hegemony and Socialist Strategy*, entitled "Articulation and Discourse," the authors argue for the "centrality" (epistemological, though they do not say so) of discourse: "If we consider social relations from the perspective of a naturalist paradigm, contradiction is excluded. But if we consider social relations as discursively constructed, contradiction becomes possible" (*HSS*, p. 110). But if we consider social relations from the point of view of Marxist materialism, contradiction is certainly not excluded either. The omission registered here in the leap from "naturalism" to the centrality of discourse is flagrant, to the point that it may be regarded as

strategic. Subsequently, in their discussion of "antagonism," Laclau and Mouffe are somewhat more forthright: they concur with Popper in regarding as "self-defeating" the assertion that "the real is contradictory." Popper's "famous critique" is apparently so decisive that it can be relegated to a footnote.

Having effectively censored classical Marxism and Leninism on this point, Laclau and Mouffe nevertheless insist rather nervously that their affirmation of "discursive practices" as the only proper alternative to the "thought/reality dichotomy" does not make them idealists:

> The fact that every object is constituted as an object of discourse has *nothing to do* with whether there is a world external to thought, or with the realism/idealism opposition. An earthquake or the falling of a brick is an event that certainly exists, in the sense that it occurs here and now, independently of my will. But whether their specificty as objects is constructed in terms of 'natural phenomena' or 'expressions of the wrath of God', depends upon the structuring of a discursive field. What is denied is not that such objects exist externally to thought, but the rather different assertion that they could constitute themselves as objects outside any discursive condition of emergence. (*HSS*, p. 108)

This is the neo-Kantian agnosticism of modern phenomenology, dressed up in the jargon of post-structuralism. The earthquake and the falling brick are allowed as "things-in-themselves," but their objective existence in no way impinges on their "specificity as objects." We could readily agree that the discourses of religion and natural science will interpret such real events quite differently, but for Laclau and Mouffe there can be no basis for determining which discourse has the stronger claim to objective validity—none, that is, except the pragmatic furthering of a specific "hegemony." The world external to thought may happen to exist for Laclau and Mouffe, but it would make no difference if it did not. Such a philosophy, in the words of Ellen Meiksins Wood, "entails not only the dissolution of social reality into discourse, but a denial of *history* and the logic of the historical process." (*The Retreat from Class*, p. 62.).

The dialectical materialist argument against such exercises in "bracketing," which goes back at least to Engels's *Anti-Duehring*, is, it seems, simply a "prejudice" at whose "root . . . lies an assumption of the *mental* character of discourse." "Against this," Laclau and Mouffe, "will affirm the *material* character of every discursive structure" (*HSS*, p. 108). But, as any reader of Marxist philosophy knows, Marxist dialectical materialism also "affirms" the *material* character of discursive structures, without being forced to deny that they are mental, i.e., "thinking matter." In a manner reminiscent of cold war ideologues like Popper and Sidney Hook, Laclau and Mouffe "refute" this position by simply misrepresenting it—in this case as a mind/matter dualism. As support for their affirmation of the materiality of discourse—which is a roundabout way of denying materiality to *objects* except as they enter into discourse—Laclau and Mouffe cite the "theory of speech acts," specifically Wittgenstein's theory of language games:

> It is evident that the very material properties of objects are part of what Wittgenstein calls language game, which is an example of what we have called discourse. What constitutes a differential position, and therefore a relational identity with certain linguistic elements, is not the idea of a building stone or a slab as such. (The connection with the idea of 'building stone' has not, as far as we know, been sufficient to construct any building.) The linguistic and non-linguistic elements are not merely juxtaposed, but constitute a differential and structured system of positions—that is, a discourse. The differential positions include, therefore, a dispersion of very diverse material elements. (*HSS*, p. 108)

If Laclau and Mouffe are saying anything at all in this, beyond the proposition that buildings are not built without some discursive mediation, it is that the actual material properties of things are constituted in accordance with the overall system of structured linguistic differences into which they enter in the course of performative discourse. The real properties of stone slabs, then, have no existence— or at least, no knowable existence—outside the request "slab." And this is meant to prove that the belief in the centrality (primacy) of discourse is in all ways consistent with materialism. One may suppose that even Wittgenstein would have had the honesty and good sense to denounce such a piece of pseudoreasoning. Against this, a consistent materialist might usefully refer to the theory of signs advanced by V. N. Voloshinov: "Signs also are particular, material things . . . ." *Marxism and the Philosophy of Language*, trans. Ladislav Matejka and I. R. Titunik [New York: Seminar Press, 1973], p. 10).

16. "The silent question running throughout the Laclau-Mouffe argument is: who will be the bearer of discourse? Who will constitute the relevant social identities? Or, to put it another way, in the words of Mouffe and Laclau themselves: 'who is the articulating subject'? That is, not only who will generate the 'hegemonic' discourse, but who, given the 'open and indeterminate' character of the social, will be the 'hegemonic subject' around whom the political agent will be constructed by means of 'articulatory practices'?" (Wood, *The Retreat from Class*, p. 63).

17. Ernesto Laclau, "The Politics and Limits of Modernity," in *Universal Abandon? The Politics of Postmodernism*, ed. Andrew Ross (Minneapolis: University of Minnesota Press, 1988).

18. "And so art is everywhere, since artifice is at the heart of reality. And so art is dead, not only because its critical transcendence is gone, but because reality itself, entirely impregnated by an aesthetic which is unseparable from its own structure, has been confused with its own image" (Jean Baudrillard, "The Orders of Simulacra," in *Simulations*, trans. Paul Foss, Paul Patton, and Philip Beitchman [New York: Semiotext(e), 1983], pp. 151–52).

19. Karl Marx, *The Eighteenth Brumaire of Louis Bonaparte* (Beijing: Foreign Languages Press, 1978), pp. 13–14.

20. Wood, *The Retreat from Class*, p. 62.

21. Ibid., pp. 116–29.

22. T. W. Adorno, *Aesthetic Theory*, trans. C. Lenhart (London: Routledge Kegan Paul, 1984), p. 33.

23. Samir Amin, *Class and Nation, Historically and in the Current Crisis* (New York: Monthly Review Press, 1980), p. 2.

24. See Amin, *Class and Nation*, pp. 184–89.

25. See Angel Rama, *La transculturación narrativa en América Latina (Mexico: Siglo veintiuno, 1982)*.

26. See Manlio Argueta, *One Day of Life*, trans. Bill Brow (New York: Vintage, 1983), and *Cuzcatlán: Where the Southern Sea Beats*, trans. Clark Hansen (New York: Vintage, 1987), and Eduardo Galeano, *Memory of Fire*, trans. Cedric Belfrage (New York: Pantheon, 1985–88) vols. 1–3.

27. Miguel Barnet, "La novela testimonio: Socio-literatura" in *Testimonio y literatura*, ed. René Jara and Hernán Vidal (Minneapolis: Institute for the Study of Ideologies and Literature, 1985) p. 288; translation mine.

28. See George Yúdice, "Marginality and the Ethics of Survival," in *Universal Abandon?*

29. Enrique Dussel, *Philosophy of Liberation*, trans. Aquilina Martínez and Christine Morkovsky (1980; Maryknoll, N.Y.: Orbis Books, 1985); hereafter cited as *PL*.

30. This Hegelian concept of dialectics is openly and falsely attributed to Marx: "For his part Marx, in the few pages on the method of political economy in the *Grundrisse*, describes the dialectical method as the movement that 'ascends from the abstract to the concrete' . . . until it reaches the simplest category . . . [,] which is nothing less that the foundation of the totality" (*PL*, p. 157). Dussel neglects to add here that this totality is, for Marx, still only a "totality of thoughts" and that Marx specifically criticizes Hegel in this passage for equating such a "totality of thoughts"—the approximation of the concrete in thinking—with the real itself. See Marx, *Grundrisse*, pp. 100–102.

31. Concurrent with this casual dismissal of dialectics there is in Dussel's work a familiar attempt to preserve the discursive suggestion of materialism while its basic philosophical content is discarded. Dussel is, however, uncharacteristically explicit in his argument: "Naive cosmological or acritical materialism," he writes, "affirms that everything is matter. . . . All reality arises by differ-

entiation from the original identity of matter. In this case, everything is internal to matter; there is no freedom or responsibility; determination and necessity reign supreme." (*PL*, pp. 102–3). This "naive" materialism is, then, erroneously attributed to Engels's *The Dialectic of Nature*. The substantive arguments of dialectical materialism are here, as in *Hegemony and Socialist Strategy*, carefully distorted. Meanwhile, according to "authentic . . . or critical materialism . . . things are relevant inasmuch as *with them* . . . are fabricated things needed by the other as such, beyond the present system of necessity" (*PL* p. 103). Here, perhaps, Dussel has not gone so far as to equate material objects with "differential positions within discourse"; instead, we are presented with a pragmatism tinged with mystical Christianity. A thing is finally just a "sense-thing" that is made "relevant" by an ontologically prior subject, one which Dussel portrays in the deceptively concrete guise of a "culture."

32. See Roberto Fernández Retamar, *Para una teoría de la literatura hispanoamericana* (Havana: Casa de las Américas, 1975); see also Retamar, *Caliban and Other Essays*, trans. Edward Baker et al. (Minneapolis, University of Minnesota Press, 1989).

33. Retamar, *Para una teoría*, p. 45; my translation.

34. See Desiderio Navarro, "Eurocentrismo y anti-eurocentrismo en la teoría literaria de América Latina y Europa," *Revista de crítica latinoamericana* 8, no. 16 (1982): 7–26.

35. "Spatially central, the *ego cogito* constituted the periphery." (*PL*, p. 3).

36. V. I. Lenin, "Conspectus of Hegel's Book *The Science of Logic*," in *Collected Works* (Moscow: Progress Publishers, 1981), 38: 109.

37. See Fredric Jameson, "Postmodernism, or, The Cultural Logic of Late Capitalism," *New Left Review*, no. 146 (1984): 53–92.

38. Alfred Sohn-Rethel, *Intellectual and Manual Labour: A Critique of Epistemology*, trans. Martin Sohn-Rethel (Atlantic Highlands, N.J.: Humanities Press, 1978), p. xii.

39. See Perry Anderson, *Considerations of Western Marxism* (London: Verso, 1976).

40. Barbara Foley has recently observed that the current enthusiasm of the New Left for "radical democracy" and its assertion of the "outmodedness" of class-based oppositional movements can be traced back to the "Popular Front against Fascism" line adopted by the Comintern in the 1930s: "[F]uller investigation into the Popular Front will reveal the peculiar irony that the revisionist abandonment of a class analysis in fact originated during this period." See Barbara Foley, "Marxism in the Poststructuralist Moment: Some Notes on the Problem of Revising Marx," *Cultural Critique* (forthcoming).

Chapter 1

1. Fredric Jameson, Afterword to *Aesthetics and Politics*, by Theodor Adorno, Walter Benjamin, Ernst Bloch, Bertolt Brecht, and Georg Lukács, trans. and ed. Ronald Taylor (London: NLB, 1977), p. 196; hereafter cited as *AP*.

2. Theodor Adorno, *Minima Moralia*, trans. E. F. N. Jephcott (London: NLB, 1974), p. 143.

3. Ibid., p. 144.

4. The phrase is from Gillian Rose, *The Melancholy Science: An Introduction to the Thought of Theodor W. Adorno* (New York: Columbia University Press, 1978).

5. Fredric Jameson, "Reification and Utopia in Mass Culture," *Social Text* 1, no. 1 (1979): 130–48.

6. Tony Bennett, *Formalism and Marxism* (London: Methuen, 1979), p. 148.

7. See ibid., pp. 167–68.

8. Georg Lukács, *The Theory of the Novel*, trans. Anna Bostock (Cambridge; Mass.: MIT Press, 1971), p. 21.

9. See Alfred Sohn-Rethel, *Intellectual and Manual Labour: A Critique of Epistemology*, trans. Martin Sohn-Rethel (Atlantic Highlands, N.J.: Humanities Press, 1978), p. xii.

10. Ibid., p. xii.

11. Karl Marx, *The Eighteenth Brumaire of Louis Bonaparte* (Beijing: Foreign Languages Press, 1978), p. 39; hereafter cited as *EB*.

12. Karl Marx, *Der achtzehnte Brumaire des Louis Bonaparte* (Berlin: Dietz Verlag, 1984), p. 19.

13. Karl Marx, *Class Struggles in France, 1848–1850* (New York: International Publishers, 1964), p. 33.

14. Max Horkheimer and Theodor W. Adorno, *Dialectic of Enlightenment*, trans., John Cumming (New York: Seabury Press, 1972), p. 26; my emphasis.

15. Ezra Pound, "Moeurs Contemporaines," in *Personae* (New York: New Directions, 1971), p. 181.

16. Horkheimer and Adorno, *Dialectic of Enlightenment*, p. xii.

17. In particular, those charges made by Jeffrey Mehlman in *Revolution and Repetition* (Berkeley and Los Angeles: University of California Press, 1977).

18. Ibid., p. 16.

19. Karl Marx, *Grundrisse* trans. Martin Nicolaus (New York: Vintage, 1973), pp.449–50; hereafter cited as *G*.

20. Sohn-Rethel, *Intellectual and Manual Labour*, p. 119.

21. Karl Marx and Frederick Engels, *The German Ideology* (New York: International Publishers, 1978). See, for example: "The only connection which still links them [i.e., "abstract individuals"] with the productive forces and with their own existence—labour—has lost all semblance of self-activity and only sustains their life by stunting it" (p. 92).

Chapter 2

1. The "Maximilian and Carlotta" episode has been the subject of innumerable literary and quasi-literary portrayals. As early as 1868 the Mexican author Juan Antonio Mateos, evidently still pro-imperialist in his sentiments, had published his *novela histórica, El cerro de las campanas (memorias de un guerrillero)* (Mexico City, 1868). Various *corridos*, or Mexican folk ballads, which treat the subject with a curious blend of nationalism and imperial nostalgia, have been recorded, e.g., "Corrido de Maximiliano de Austria" and "Adiós a mamá Carlota," in *El corrido popular en el Estado de México*, ed. Mario Colín (Mexico City: Biblioteca del Estado de México, 1972) 41–49; and "Corrido del Emperador Maximiliano" in *El corrido mexicano*, ed. Vicente T. Mendoza (Mexico City: Fondo de cultura económica, 1954), p. 59. Outside Mexico there has been no lack of titles, most of them now obscure. To cite only a few: the nineteenth-century Spanish author José Zorrilla's "epic" *El drama del alma* (Mexico City, 1868); Olive Tilford Dargan's "Carlotta," in *Semiramis and Other Plays* (New York: Brentano's, 1904); Maurice Rostand's *Charlotte et Maximilien, pièce en six tableaux, en prose* (Paris: Nagel, 1945); Franz Werfel's *Juarez und Maximilian: Dramatische Historie in drei Phasen und dreizehn Bilden* (Berlin: Paul Zsolnay Verlag, 1924); and Bertita Harding's *Phantom Crown: the Story of Maximilian and Carlotta of Mexico* (New York: Blue Ribbon Books, 1934). The latter two works are the source of the screenplay (authored by John Huston among others) for the 1939 Hollywood film *Juarez* starring Paul Muni in the title role, Brian Aherne as Maximilian, and Bette Davis as Carlotta and directed by William Dieterle.

2. Georges Bataille, *Manet*, trans. A. Wainhouse and J. Emmons (1955; Geneva: Skira, 1983); hereafter cited as *M*.

3. See Françoise Cachin, Introduction to *M*, p. 8.

4. Bataille clearly greets this "negation" of the anecdotal as unambiguously progressive. Painting is now "free" to confront "being" directly (see *M*, p. 63). In his excellent study, *The Painting of Modern Life: Paris in the Art of Manet and His Followers* (New York: Knopf, 1985), T. J. Clark complicates Bataille's entelechy by suggesting a link between the freedom from "anecdotes" and the more immediate object of (post-) representation for Manet and the impressionists: the newly "gentrified" setting produced by Hausmann's overhaul of Paris. "They [the impressionists] see it [Paris as

the setting of "modern life"] as a space from which mere anecdote and narrative have been displaced at last, and which therefore is paintable, but do they not mean by anecdote and narrative simply the presence—the pressure, the influence—of other classes besides their own?" (p. 23).

5. Nils Gösta Sandblad, *Manet: Three Studies in Artistic Conception*, trans. Walter Nash, Publications of the New Society of Letters at Lund; no. 46 (Lund: C. W. K. Gleerup, 1954); hereafter cited as *MTS*.

6. For a discussion of the influence of mass journalism on painting, see Edward Baker, "Painting the News: Picasso's *Guernica*," and René Jara, "Reading the News in Painting: Picasso's *Guernica*," in *Ideologies and Literature* 3, no. 14 (1980): 85–94.

7. Walter Benjamin, "The Storyteller," in *Illuminations*, trans. Harry Zohn (New York: Schocken Books, 1969). See also T. J. Clark, who, without invoking Benjamin, makes much the same point regarding Manet's *Olympia*: "[I]nstead of the fictive body on the bed, a more limited fiction called 'the picture' was consumed and imagined—it seemed the best on offer. Yet even this fact is open to contrary interpretations, and eager discussion of 'the free play of the signifier' may on the whole be premature. It is true that *Olympia* makes hay with our assumptions as spectators, and may lead us to doubt the existence on canvas of three dimensions, the female body, and other minds; *but this very negation is pictured as something produced in the social order, happening as part of an ordinary exchange of goods and services"* (*The Painting of Modern Life*, p. 80; my emphasis).

8. These lithographs have been reproduced in Antonio Arriaga Ochoa, ed., *La patria recobrada: Estampas de México y los mexicanos durante la intervención francesa* (Mexico City: Fondo de cultura económica, 1967), p. 210.

9. See Benjamin, "On Some Motifs in Baudelaire," in *Illuminations*, p. 159.

10. The daguerreotype is reproduced in Arriaga, *La patria recobrada*, p. 246.

11. "[T]he *Execution of Maximilian* parts company with the newspaper account of the tragic [*sic*] events at Querétaro. . . . [T]he picture *obliterates* the text, *and the meaning of the picture is not in the text behind it but in the obliteration of that text"* (*M*, p. 62).

12. *The Barricade* is reproduced in *MTS*, pl. 56.

13. See T. J. Clark, *The Absolute Bourgeois: Artists and Politics in France, 1848–1851* (Princeton, N.J.: Princeton University Press, 1982).

14. See Clark, "The Picture of the Barricade," in ibid., pp. 9–30.

Chapter 3

1. Carlos Fuentes, in *La nueva novela hispanoamericana* (Mexico City: Joaquín Moritz, 1969), writes: "La obra de Juan Rulfo no es sólo la máxima expresión que ha logrado hasta ahora la novela mexicana: a través de ella podemos encontrar el hilo que nos conduce a la nueva novela latinoamericana" (pp. 16–17) (Rulfo's work is not merely the highest expression achieved by the Mexican novel thus far: through it we encounter the thread that leads to the new Latin American novel.) More recently, Julio Rodríguez-Luis has dubbed *Pedro Páramo* "la primera novela moderna latinoamericana" (the first modern American novel); see *La literatura hispanoamericana: entre el compromiso y la experimentación* (Madrid: Editorial Fundamentos, 1984), p. 233. Gabriel García Márquez, who claims to have committed *Pedro Páramo* to memory, has written recently that "el escrutinio a fondo de la obra de Juan Rulfo me dio por fin el camino que buscaba para continuar mis libros" (the profound scrutiny of Juan Rulfo's work finally showed me the path I was looking for). "No son más de 300 páginas," he adds, "pero son casi tantas, y creo que tan perdurables, como las de Sófocles" (They don't amount to more than three hundred pages, but they are as many, and as lasting, as those of Sophocles). ("Breves nostalgias sobre Juan Rulfo," in ed. Benitez Rojo, et al. *Inframundo: El México de Juan Rulfo* [Hanover, N.H.: Ediciones del Norte, 1980], p. 25). And it should come as no surprise that at least one reader has proclaimed Rulfo's "postmodernity": "[El arte de Juan Rulfo] es una muestra de literatura y pensamiento posmodernos, autoreflexivos o autoreferenciales" (Rulfo's art is an example of postmodern literature and thought—self reflexive and self-referential).

108 □ NOTES

(Jonathan Tittler, "*Pedro Páramo*: Nihilismo fracasado,") *INTI* [*Revista de literatura hispanoamericana*] 13–14 (1981): 73.

2. In a review of *Pedro Páramo* originally published in 1955, Alí Chumacero criticized what he termed "el adverso encuentro entre un estilo preponderantemente realista y una imaginación dada a lo irreal" ("El *Pedro Páramo* de Juan Rulfo," in *Recopilación de textos sobre Juan Rulfo, ed. Antonio Benítez Rojo [Havana: Casa de las Américas, 1969], p. 109).

3. See Alfonso Reyes, "Edición francesa de *Pedro Páramo*," *Vida universitaria* [Monterrrey, Mexico] 9 (1959); Carlos Fuentes, in *La nueva novela hispanoamericana*, pp. 19–27, and, more recently, in "Rulfo, el tiempo del mito," in *Inframundo*, pp. 11–21; and Octavio Paz, "Paisaje y novela en México," in *Corriente alterna* (Mexico City: Siglo Veintiuno, 1967), pp. 16–18.

4. George Ronald Freeman's *Paradise and Fall in Rulfo's "Pedro Páramo": Archetype and Structural Unity* (Cuernavaca: Centro Intercultural de Documentación, 1970) is the standard myth-critical reading. Linguistic analysis of Rulfo is to be found in such monographs as Nila Gutiérrez Marrone's *El estilo de Juan Rulfo: Estudio lingüístico* (New York: Bilingual Press, 1978), and Raúl Rivadeneira Prada's *Rulfo en llamas: un análisis comunicacional de "El llano en llamas" y Pedro Páramo* (La Paz: Editorial Difusión, 1980). Structuralist readings abound; the standard seems to be Hugo Rodríguez Alcalá's *El arte de Juan Rulfo* (Mexico City: Instituto de Bellas Artes, 1965). Violetta Peralta and Liliana Befumo Boschi's *Rulfo: La soledad creadora* (Buenos Aires: Fernando García Cambeiro, 1975) rounds things out with a hermeneutic interpretation, in the manner of Cassirer and Ricoeur.

5. Carlos Blanco Aguinaga, "Realidad y estilo de Juan Rulfo," in *Recopilación de textos sobre Juan Rulfo*; hereafter cited in the text.

6. *Lo real maravilloso* is borrowed, as Carpentier carefully acknowledges, from the Haitian author Jacques Stephen Alexis.

7. Alejo Carpentier, "Prólogo" (1949), in *El reino de este mundo* (Buenos Aires: América nueva, 1974), p. 9; my translation; hereafter cited as "P."

8. Walter Benjamin, "Surrealism," in *Reflections*, trans. Edmund Jephcott (New York: Harcourt Brace Jovanovich, 1978).

9. See "Los muertos no tienen tiempo ni espacio: Diálogo con Juan Rulfo," in *La narrativa de Juan Rulfo: Interpretaciones críticas*, ed. Jospeh Sommers (Mexico City: Secretaría de Educación Pública, 1974).

10. See, for example, "El lenguaje popular como recurso estilístico," pt. 4 of Gutiérrez Marrone's *El estilo de Juan Rulfo*, in which Rulfo's stylized peasant idiolect is contrasted to the transcripts of recordings of rural *jaliscienses* taken from Oscar Lewis's *Pedro Martínez*.

11. Luis Harss, "Juan Rulfo, o la pena sin nombre," in *Recopilación de textos sobre Juan Rulfo*, p. 20; my translation.

12. Angel Rama, *Transculturación narrativa en América Latina* (Mexico City: Siglo 21, 1982), 52; my translation; hereafter cited as *T*.

13. Juan Rulfo, "La Cuesta de las Comadres," in *Obra Completa* (Caracas: Biblioteca Ayacucho, 1977). For an English translation, see Juan Rulfo, "The Hill of the Comadres," in *"The Burning Plain" and Other Stories*, trans. George D. Schade (Austin, Tex.: University of Texas Press, 1967), pp. 15–24.

14. Rulfo, "La Cuesta de las Comadres," p. 10; my translation.

15. Ibid., p. 13; translation, Schade, "The Hill of the Comadres," p. 24.

16. See Mikhail Bakhtin, "Discourse in Dostoevsky," in *Problems of Dostoevsky's Poetics*, ed. and trans. Caryl Emerson (Minneapolis: University of Minnesota Press, 1984), pp. 187–88.

17. Ibid., pp. 187–88.

18. See Vicente T. Mendoza, ed., *El corrido mexicano* (Mexico City: Fondo de Cultura Económica, 1954); hereafter cited in the text.

19. See here Walter J. Ong, *Orality and Literacy: The Technologizing of the Word* (London: Methuen, 1982): "Romances are the product of chirographic culture, creations in a new written genre heavily reliant on oral modes of thought and expression, but not consciously imitating earlier oral forms as the 'art" epic did. Popular ballads, as the Border ballads in English and Scots, develop on the edge of orality" (p. 159).

20. See Walter Benjamin, "The Storyteller," in *Illuminations*, trans. Harry Zohn (New York: Schocken Books, 1969).

21. M. M. Bakhtin and P. N. Medvedev, *The Formal Method in Literary Scholarship*, trans. Albert J. Wehrle (Baltimore: Johns Hopkins University Press, 1978), p. 181n. 26.

22. For a review of these debates (as well as an Althuserian and "nonreductionist" defense of populism), see Ernesto Laclau, "Towards a Theory of Populism," in *Politics and Ideology in Marxist Theory* (London: NLB, 1977). See also Robert Albritton et al., "Populism and Popular Ideologies," in *LARU [Latin American Research Unit] Studies* 3, nos. 2–3 (1980): 48–63.

23. See Antonio Gramsci, *Selections from the Prison Notebooks*, ed. and trans. Quintin Hoare and Geoffrey Nowell Smith (New York: International Publishers, 1971).

24. "The spoken word forms human beings into close knit groups. When a speaker is addressing an audience, the members of the audience normally become a unity, with themselves and the speaker" (Ong, *Orality and Literacy*, p. 74.)

25. See Benjamin, "The Storyteller."

26. Luis González y González records several such instances of popular reprisals against offending *bandoleros* in his local history, *Pueblo en vilo: Microhistoria de San José de Gracia* (Mexico City: El Colegio de México, 1968).

27. B. Traven, *The Cotton Pickers*, (1956; London: Allison & Busby, 1979).

28. Robert Fossaert, *La société; Une théorie générale* (Paris: Editions du Seuil, 1977), 138; my translation.

29. Alfred Sohn-Rethel, *Intellectual and Manual Labour: A Critique of Epistemology*, trans., Martin Sohn-Rethel (Atlantic Highlands, N.J.: Humanities Press, 1978), p. xii.

Chapter 4

1. Antonio Gramsci, *Selections from the Prison Notebooks*, ed. and trans. Quintin Hoare and Geoffrey Nowell Smith (New York: International Publishers, 1971), p. 52.

2. See Guillermo A. O'Donnell, *Modernización y autoritarismo* (Buenos Aires: Paidós, 1972).

3. "The nation is the discourse of the state" (Robert Fossaert, La société: Une théorie générale [Paris: Editions du Seuil, 1977), p. 138; my translation.

4. See Tony Bennett, "Text, Readers, Reading Formations," *MMLA* 16; no. 1 (Spring 1983): 3–17.

5. Octavio Paz, *The Labyrinth of Solitude*, trans. Lysander Kemp (New York: Grove Press, 1961), pp. 65–66; hereafter cited in the text.

6. Oswald de Andrade, "Manifesto Antropófago," in *Obras completas* (Rio de Janeiro: Editora Civilizaċào Brasileira, 1972) 6: 15; my translation.

7. Ibid., 6:16; my translation.

8. Benedito Nunes, Preface to *Obras completas*, by Oswald de Andrade, 6: xiv; my translation.

9. "Thus, for example, nothing more open to foreign influences than the *modernismo* of 1922, which meanwhile transformed our popular reality into an active element of Brazilian culture" (Roberto Schwarz, "Cuidado com as ideologias alienígenas (repostas a *Movimento*)," in *Pai de família* (Rio de Janeiro: Editora Paz e Terra, 1978), p. 115; my translation.

10. Karl Marx, *Grundrisse* trans. Martin Nicolaus (New York: Vintage Books, 1973, p. 90.

11. Ibid., p. 89.

12. Oswald de Andrade, *Memorias sentimentais de João Miramar* (São Paulo: Difusão Europeio do Livro, 1964) p. 56.

13. See my "*João Miramar: A Fond Memory of Brazilian Culture Industry?*" *Mester* 12, no. 2 (Fall 1984): 49–54.

14. Paulo Prado's *Retrato do Brasil*, published in 1926, attributed the backwardness of Brazil to the evils of *luxuria* (excessive and relaxed sexuality), *cobiça* (greed), and *preguiça* (laziness).

15. Randal Johnson and Robert Stam, "The Shape of Brazilian Film History," *Brazilian Cinema*, ed. Johnson and Stam, (Toronto: Associated University Press, 1982), p. 20.

16. Walter Benjamin, "The Work of Art in the Age of Mechanical Reproduction," *Illuminations*, trans. Harry Zohn (New York: Schocken Books, 1969), p. 234.

17. Ibid., p. 233.

18. Ibid., p. 240.

19. As early as 1950, Antonio Candido, attempting to explain a noticeable falling off after the explosive surge of literary culture in the 1930s and 1940s, suggested that this had less to do with the gradual exhaustion of literary imaginations than with the sudden introduction of *novos meios de comunicaçao* (new means of communication) that were able to establish more direct contact with the increasingly numerous cultural consumers:

> One saw then that at the very moment at which Brazilian literature had successfully forged a certain literary tradition, had created a certain system of expression that linked it to the past and opened paths to the future—at this moment the literary traditions begin to cease functioning as stimuli. In effect, written forms of expression entered into a relative crisis in the face of competition from means of expression either new or newly redeployed—for instance, radio, film, current drama, dime novels. Before the consolidation of classroom instruction could assure the dissemination of a, so to speak, *literary literature*, these vehicles, thanks to the spoken word, the image, the sound, and so forth, made it possible for an ever-increasing number of people to share with the utmost convenience in that ration of dream and emotion that used to guarantee to the book its traditional prestige. And for those whom a certain tradition excluded, the book presented limitations which these new avenues surpassed, by lowering the need for intellectual concentration. See *Literatura e sociedade; Estudos de teoria e historia literaria* [São Paulo: Editora Nacional, 1965], p. 137; my translation)

20. See Randal Johnson, "Cinema Novo and Cannibalism: *Macunaima*" *Brazilian Cinema*, pp. 178–90.

21. Joaquim Pedro de Andrade, "Cannibalism and Self-Cannibalism," *Brazilian Cinema*, pp. 82-83.

22. Joaquim Pedro de Andrade, interviewed by Alex Viany, in "Criticism and Self-Criticism," *Brazilian Cinema*, p. 74.

23. Johnson, "Cinema Novo and Cannibalism: *Macunaima*," pp. 178, 190.

24. T. W. Adorno, to Walter Benjamin, 18 March, 1936, "Letters to Walter Benjamin," in *Aesthetics and Politics*, trans. and Ronald Taylor (London: NLB, 1977), p. 123.

25. Max Horkheimer and T. W. Adorno, *Dialectic of Enlightenment*, trans. John Cumming (New York: Seabury Press, 1972), p. 158.

26. Quoted in Schwarz, "Nota sobre vanguarda e conformisimo," *Pai de familia*, p. 47 my translation.

27. Ibid.; my translation.

28. Schwarz, "Cultura e política: 1964–1969," in *Pai de familia*, p. 62; my translation.

29. Ibid., p. 76; my translation.

30. Ibid., p. 77; my translantion.

31. See Karl Marx, *Capital, vol. 2, The Process of Circulation of Capital* ed. Frederick Engels (New York: International Publishers, 1967).

32. See Glauber Rocha, "An Aesthetic of Hunger," trans. Randal Johnson and Burnes Hollyman, *Brazilian Cinema*, pp. 69- 71.

33. Randal Johnson and Robert Stam, "The Cinema of Hunger: Nelson Pereira dos Santos' *Vidas secas*," in *Brazilian Cinema*, p. 126 p. 126.

Index

Index

Theory and History of Literature

Neil Larsen is associate professor of Spanish and Latin American literature at Northeastern University. He received his M.A. and Ph.D. in comparative literature from the University of Minnesota. Larsen edited the monograph *The Discourse of Power: Culture, Hegemony, and the Authoritarian State in Latin America*, and contributes to *Ideologies and Literature*, *Revista Iberoamericana*, and *Hispamérica*.